Organic Container Gardening

Grow Pesticide-Free Fruits and Vegetables
in Small Spaces

Second Edition

Barbara Barker

Prairie Oak Publishing
Maryville, Missouri

Organic Container Gardening is written for informational purposes only. It is not intended to diagnose, treat, cure, prescribe, or prevent any medical condition or replace the advice of a licensed health practitioner.

Organic Container Gardening is not intended to provide all information on the subject matter covered. While every effort has been made to assure the accuracy of this book, there may be mistakes in content and typography. The authors and publisher assume no responsibility or liability with respect to any alleged or real damage caused, directly or indirectly, by information contained in this book. Inclusion of company names, contact information, web sites, product names, and other resources do not represent endorsements by the authors or publisher. If you do not want to be bound by this disclaimer, you may return this book to the publisher for a full refund.

Copyright © 2009, 2011 by Barbara Barker.
All Rights Reserved. First edition published as *Container Gardening for Health* in 2009
Second edition 2011

ISBN 978-0-9786293-6-6

Library of Congress Control Number: 2011935627
Library of Congress Subject Headings:
Container gardening
Organic gardening
Pesticide residues in food

1.0

Prairie Oak Publishing
221 South Saunders St.
Maryville MO 64468
www.PrairieOakPublishing.com

For Richard, Rhett, and Brian

Acknowledgements

Richard Barker, my husband, deserves more than thanks for all he has done for me. In regards to this book, his companionship in the garden and his editing assistance are especially appreciated. Rhett and Brian, my children, have been my garden buddies since they could walk. They are also my go-to people for bug identification. Thank you, Richard, Rhett and Brian, for encouraging me to write this book and allowing me the time to write it.

Thank you to my sister, Bonnie Nelson, for giving me the idea behind this book and the confidence to write it.

I would also like to thank my mother, Rita Ramsey, who has encouraged me to write since I was a little girl.

My friends, Leslie Kurtz, and Jim and B O'Toole of O'Toole's Herb Farm inspired me to garden organically. Thank you.

Finally, I would like to thank my publisher, Jeff Goettemoeller, for believing in my writing, for encouraging me along the way, and for demonstrating remarkable patience throughout the book writing process.

Contents

List of Figures – 8
Introduction – 9

1. **Chemical Residue on Your Food** – 11
2. **The Forbidden Apple** – 15
   Nutritional Information for Apples – 15
   Residues found on Apples – 16
   Dwarf Apple Varieties and Chill Hours – 16, 17
   Planting Dates, Location, and Moisture for Apple Trees – 18
   Temperature, Container Choice, Soil, and Planting Apple Trees – 18, 19
   Fertilization, Pests, and Diseases of Apple Trees – 19, 20
   Pruning Apple Trees – 20
   Harvesting and Storage of Apples – 22
3. **Celery** – 23
   Nutritional Information for Celery – 23
   Residues found on Celery – 24
   Varieties of Cutting Celery and Stalk Celery – 24
   Planting Dates and Container Choice for Celery – 25
   Optimum Growing Conditions and Soil for Celery – 25
   Growing Instructions and Starting Celery from Seed – 25, 26
   Fertilization, Harvesting, Use, and Storage of Celery – 26, 27
4. **Strawberries, Mother Nature's Candy** – 29
   Nutritional Information for Strawberries – 29
   Residues found on Strawberries – 30
   June Bearing, Day Neutral, Alpine, and Everbearing Varieties – 31
   Planting Dates for Strawberries – 31, 32
   Location and Container Choice for Strawberries – 32, 33
   Optimum Growing Conditions for Strawberries – 33
   Propagating Strawberries from Seed, Divisions, and Runners – 34, 35
   Soil, Fertilization and Soil pH for Strawberry Plants – 35, 36
   Pests and Diseases on Strawberries – 36
   Harvesting and Storage of Strawberries – 36, 37
5. **Peaches and Nectarines** – 39
   Nutritional Information for Peaches – 39
   Residues found on Peaches – 40

      Dwarf Peach and Nectarine Varieties and Planting Dates – 40, 41
      Location for Peaches – 42
      Watering, Temperature, Frost Protection, and Chill Hours – 42
      Container Choice and Preparation – 42
      Purchasing Peach Trees, Soil and Planting – 43, 44
      Fertilization, Pests and Diseases of Peach Trees – 44, 45
      Pruning Peach Trees – 45, 46
      Thinning Fruit and Harvesting Peach Trees – 46

6. Spinach – 47

      Nutritional Information for Spinach – 47
      Residues found on Spinach – 48
      Varieties, Planting Dates, and Warm Weather Spinach Substitutes – 48
      Container Choice, Planting Procedure, & Optimum Growing Conditions – 49
      Pests, Diseases, Soil, and Troubleshooting Spinach – 50
      Harvesting, Storage, and Extending the Spinach Season – 50, 51
      Safe Handling of Produce from the Garden – 52

7. Grapes – 53

      Nutritional Information for Grapes – 53
      Residues found on Grapes – 54
      Varieties, Temperature, Pollinator Requirements, & Planting Dates – 54, 55
      Container Choice, Site Selection, & Optimum Growing Conditions – 55, 56
      Soil, Planting Procedure, and Fertilization for Grapes – 56, 57
      Pests and Diseases on Grapes – 57
      Pruning Grapes – 57, 58
      Harvesting and Storage of Grapes – 58

8. Sweet Bell Peppers – 59

      Nutritional Information for Sweet Bell Peppers – 59
      Residues found on Sweet Bell Peppers – 60
      Sweet Bell Pepper Varieties and Seed Starting – 60
      Transplanting and Soil for Growing Sweet Bell Peppers – 61, 62
      Optimum Growing Conditions and Fertilization of Sweet Bell Peppers – 62
      Pests & Diseases of Sweet Bell Peppers – 62
      Harvesting Sweet Bell Peppers – 63

9. Potatoes – 65

      Nutritional Information and Solanine Toxicity for Potatoes – 65, 66
      Residues found on Potatoes – 66, 67
      Potato Varieties – 67

  Planting Dates, Container Choice, and Optimum Growing Conditions – 67
  Soil and Planting Procedure for Potatoes – 68, 69
  Fertilization, Pests, and Diseases of Potatoes – 69
  Harvesting and Storage of Potatoes – 69, 70

10. **Blueberries – 71**

  Nutritional Information for Blueberries – 71
  Blueberry Varieties – 71, 72
  Residues found on Blueberries – 72
  Climate and Container Choice for Blueberry Plants – 72
  Soil, Fertilization, and Moisture for Blueberry Plants – 72, 73
  Pests and Diseases on Blueberry Plants – 73
  Harvesting Blueberries – 73

11. **Lettuce – 75**

  Nutritional Information for Lettuce – 75
  Residues found on Lettuce – 76
  Crisphead, Butterhaed, Leaf, and Romaine Lettuce Varieties – 76
  Other Favorite Greens – 77
  Planting Dates and Container Choice for Lettuce – 77
  Planting Procedure & Optimum Growing Conditions for Lettuce – 77, 78
  Pests and Diseases on Lettuce – 78
  Soil, Fertilization, Harvesting and Storage of Lettuce – 78

12. **Kale – 79**

  Nutritional Information for Kale – 79
  Residues found on Kale – 79, 80
  Seed Starting, Container Choice, and Soil for Kale – 80
  Harvesting and Storage of Kale – 80
  Optimum Growing Conditions, Pests, and Diseases – 80, 81, 82

13. **Primary Pesticides Found On the Dirty Dozen – 83**

14. **Pests and Diseases – 89**

  Raised Growing Beds – 105
  Selected Resources/Bibliography – 106
  Glossary – 109
  Index – 113

Figures

Fig. 1-1. Examples of containers for plants – 10
Fig. 2-1. Young apple tree – 20
Fig. 3-1. Celery plant – 26
Fig. 4-1. Planting a terra-cotta strawberry pot – 32
Fig. 4-2. Hanging strawberry plants – 32
Fig. 4-3. Pot with water resevoir – 32
Fig. 4-4. Flat under fluorescent light – 34
Fig. 5-1. Bud union – 44
Fig. 5-2. Pruning shoots below graft union – 45
Fig. 5-3. Pruning vertical shoots – 45
Fig. 5-4. Young peach tree – 46
Fig. 5-5. Peach tree with fruit – 46
Fig. 6-1. Container spinach garden – 49
Fig. 7-1. Grape vine on chain link fence – 56
Fig. 7-2. Containerized grape vine – 58
Fig. 7-3. Muscadine grapes – 58
Fig. 8-1. Newly planted cell packs – 61
Fig. 8-2. Recycled clamshell flat – 61
Fig. 8-3. Young pepper plants in a concrete container – 61
Fig. 8-4. Containerized pepper plant – 62
Fig. 9-1. Potato shoots – 68
Fig. 11-1. Lettuce in raised growing bed – 77
Fig. 14-1. Coddling moth damage inside an apple – 90
Fig. 14-2. Japanese beetle adult – 92
Fig. 14-3. Colorado potato beetle – 93
Fig. 14-4. Colorado potato beetle larvae – 93
Fig. 14-5. Stink bug adult – 94
Fig. 14-6. Aphid adults – 95
Fig. 14-7. Leafhopper adult – 96

Introduction

In 1997, my four year old son began having seizures. Though the cause of his seizures was never determined, I learned that environmental factors could play a role. I took a hard look around and began trying to reduce the amount of chemicals in our household. I stopped using the monthly pest control service (in Florida that's a big change), had old paint removed from our windowsills and started paying closer attention to the chemicals we consumed in our diet. I'm not suggesting that any one of these factors caused my son's seizures, but I felt that it was important to reduce the overall chemical impact on my family. Perhaps nothing affects us too greatly by itself, but what of the cumulative effect of so many different chemicals on tiny bodies?

Perhaps the biggest change I made during this time was the decision to begin growing much of our own produce. I didn't have time to grow everything we ate, but I could grow a few of those produce items that had the highest residues.

I became an avid gardener, and even purchased a small seed company, The Gourmet Gardener, in 1999. Through my work, I learned that my customers were equally interested in growing healthy produce for their families. But unlike me, most of my customers didn't have five acres to grow elaborate gardens. With sales of dwarf citrus and berries skyrocketing, I began to look at what other produce could grow well in containers. I discovered that all the produce generally recognized as having the highest residue levels could be grown in containers or in a small garden space.

This book provides a container/small garden guide for growing each of the items on the list of high residue produce (see list on page 13). You need not grow all the items on the list to reduce your family's chemical impact. Just selecting the three items that you consume most often will significantly reduce your family's exposure.

Fig. 1-1: Examples of containers for plants

Chapter 1

CHEMICAL RESIDUE ON YOUR FOOD

The EPA and USDA have a treasure trove of data regarding pesticide use and residue on fruits and vegetables. They even have a database listing the "tolerance levels" allowed for each chemical on our food. But they can't tell us the cumulative effect of all the residues in our diets. Even in baby foods, some levels of pesticides are tolerated. The truth is, no one really knows how our health will be impacted by the total chemical burden we place on our bodies. I only know I don't want my family to consume malathion and organophosphates with our green beans.

This book shows how to grow certain foods organically—those that typically have the highest pesticide residues. I do occasionally use pesticides in my garden, but I know what I'm putting on my food and I know what residues I'm willing to tolerate for my family.

Some chemicals are worse than others. Unfortunately, food at the grocery store isn't labeled "Captan" or "Organophosphates." Unless we are willing to shell out extra cash for the organic label, we are expected to eat whatever is offered with no knowledge as to the chemicals we are eating.

Even if the government did require labeling, I'm not sure I would trust the labels, given that much of our food originates in other countries. In the course of researching this book, for example, I was stunned to learn that many vegetables imported into the U.S. have DDT residue.[1] While it may have its place in controlling malaria in foreign coun-

---

1. Agency for Toxic Substances and Disease Registry (ATSDR, An agency of the U.S. Department of Health and Human Services), "Public Health Statement for DDT, DDE, and DDD," (September 2002), section 1.6, http://www.atsdr.cdc.gov/PHS/PHS.asp?id=79&tid=20

tries, we've known for many years that DDT has serious health consequences for humans and wildlife.

Before continuing, I should clarify a few terms:

- When I refer to "vegetables" or "produce," I refer to both vegetables and fruits. I don't want to confuse you by interchanging the words but I don't want to bore you with extra words either.
- When I refer to "pesticides," I'm also referring to Algicides, Antifouling agents, Antimicrobials, Disinfectants and Sanitizers, Fungicides, Fumigants, Herbicides, Insecticides, Miticides (acaricides), Microbial pesticides, Molluscicides, Nematicides, Ovicides, Pheromones, Repellents, Rodenticides, Defoliants, Desiccants, Insect Growth Regulators, and Plant Growth Regulators. Whew! I'll be more specific when necessary, but in general you should know that pesticides are not the only chemicals on your food.[2]

The FDA and Center for Food Safety and Applied Nutrition compiled data into a Total Diet Study (TDS) that is commonly called the "Market Basket Study." With a desire to begin to quantify the cumulative and combined levels of pesticides fed to children, they analyzed residues on commonly eaten prepared foods. This book relies on this and other EPA and USDA studies. I don't profess to be an expert on pesticides, however, and I encourage you to research this information in greater detail.[3]

In 1988, The National Research Council was commissioned by the U.S. Congress to study issues concerning pesticides in the diets of infants and children. The results of this study are published in a 372-page book, *Pesticides in the Diets of Infants and Children*. The study concludes that children are uniquely susceptible to health problems from exposure to toxic pesticides because of their rapid growth. Infants and children also consume greater quantities of certain foods as a proportion of body weight. This leads to greater exposure to some pesticides.[4]

The problem with pesticides is that the quantity of a vegetable your child eats may exceed government expectations. Anyone who has children knows they go through phases where they will only eat one food or one group of foods. Since the government is not in your dining room calculating how many pounds of strawberries your tot has eaten this week, they cannot tell you if she has

---

2. If you would like to read about the distinctions of pesticides in greater detail than I offer in this book, go to this website: http://www.epa.gov/pesticides/about/types.htm

3. Read the *Total Diet Study* at: http://www.fda.gov/Food/FoodSafety/FoodContaminantsAdulteration/TotalDietStudy/

4. National Research Council, *Pesticides in the Diets of Infants and Children*, (1988), 359-363.

consumed too much of a certain pesticide. The government *can* tell you what foods have chemical residue even after they have been washed and prepared for eating. In fact, the U.S. Department of Agriculture and the US Food and Drug Administration conducted nearly 43,000 tests on produce samples from 2000–2004. The Environmental Working Group (EWG) analyzed this data and created a "simulation of thousands of consumers eating high and low pesticide diets..." Their study showed "that people can lower their pesticide exposure by almost 90% by avoiding the top twelve most contaminated fruits and vegetables and eating the least contaminated instead."[5]

The list of foods with the highest pesticide residues has changed slightly since 2009 when *Container Gardening for Health* was first published. Cherries and pears have dropped their notorious reputations and kale and blueberries are new additions to the "dirty dozen." As of 2011, the 12 most pesticide-laden fruits and vegetables, as established by USDA data, are as follows:

Rank	Fruit or Veggie	Page number in this book
1	Apples (most contaminated)	15
2	Celery	23
3	Strawberries	29
4	Peaches	39
5	Spinach	47
6	Nectarines, imported	39
7	Grapes, imported	53
8	Bell Peppers	59
9	Potatoes	65
10	Blueberries, domestic	71
11	Lettuce	75
12	Kale	79

5. http://www.ewg.org/foodnews/methodology/

Unfortunately, my kids really like to eat the foods at the top of the EWG's list. The "dirty dozen" includes a lot of fruits such as strawberries, peaches, nectarines, cherries, and apples—all foods that my children prefer over other fruits and vegetables. My kids are picky enough! While I don't want them to eat pesticides with their fruit, neither am I content to further limit their diets from the wholesome produce they are most likely to eat.

After talking with other parents, I realized we all wanted an inexpensive way to feed our children more foods with less pesticide residue. None of us had time and few of us had the space to grow large gardens. I began researching the problem and soon realized a family's intake of pesticides could be substantially reduced by selecting their favorite foods from the EWG's Dirty Dozen list and growing these in containers or small space gardens.

An average strawberry plant, for example, produces one quart of strawberries. Just a few pots hanging from your patio can keep you in strawberries for most of the year. An ever expanding variety of dwarf fruit trees make it possible to grow cherries, peaches, nectarines, and apples in many regions outside the typical grow zones.

Growing a few pots of your family's favorite fruits and vegetables is not only healthy, it's enjoyable. Watching fruit ripen on the vine provides almost unbearable excitement for small children. There are many lessons to teach children through gardening as well. Patience and long term gratification are at the top of this list.

So that is what this book is about: growing fruits and vegetables for your family using only organic pesticides and fertilizers. You'll find it takes very little time or space and, in addition to peace of mind, you'll gain a fun activity for the whole family.

Chapter 2

THE FORBIDDEN APPLE

It's been a long time since humans were in the Garden of Eden, but it appears we are still not supposed to eat the apple. Apples placed first on the Environmental Working Group's (EWG) list of produce containing high pesticide residues.

After viewing the results of the USDA studies, you may decide to buy organic apples at the store. This would be a better choice than purchasing conventional apples, but still not as good a choice as growing your own. The Consumers Union analyzed pesticide residue test results from the USDA's Pesticide Data Program, the Marketplace Surveillance Program of the California Department of Pesticide Regulation, and their own private tests

Pesticide Residue Ranking: #1

Nutritional Information

One medium apple with the skin on contains about 80 calories and is an excellent source of fiber, pectin, potassium, vitamin C, and antioxidants.

USDA National Nutrient Database for Standard Reference, Release 20 (2007).

Botanical Name

Malus Pumila
Family: *Rosaceae*

and found organically grown samples consistently had far fewer residues than commercially grown apples. However, pesticide residues were found in 6%–51% of organically grown samples depending on the organization conducting the tests and the specific produce being tested.[6]

Additionally, much of the organic produce available in stores is shipped great distances—often from countries outside the U.S. Long-distance shipping generally requires early harvesting and long storage times, reducing the nutritional value of apples. Fresh and homegrown is best!

General Information about Apples

Flowers of an apple tree are rosaceous (apples are members of the rose family). Those with single blooms have five petals. Those with double blooms have ten petals. Some varieties produce fruit and flowers only every other year. Leaves are oval with small serrations and alternate on the branch. Apple trees set fruit in spring or summer and ripen in late summer or fall. Fruit size can be up to 4″ in diameter. When an apple tree variety produces fruit smaller than 2″ in diameter (at harvest), it is classified as a crab apple. Bark on apple trees is brown and scaly. Apple trees are pollinated by bees and other insects.

---

6. http://www.consumersunion.org/food/organicsumm.htm

Residue

Apples sampled by the USDA (1996) were "washed and prepared for eating" before testing and yet most of the conventionally grown apples tested contained at least four pesticides. Ninety two percent of apples contained two or more pesticide residues.[7] Before your apple was picked from its tree, it was most likely sprayed by a soil fumigant at flower budding time, a fungicide to ward off apple scab and mildew, a pesticide to guard against coddling moth and bull's eye rot (twice), an herbicide (twice), chemicals to reduce fruit set and other chemicals to prevent early apple drop, and sprayed yet again with a color promoter. To prevent scald, apples are then often dipped in additional chemicals prior to cold storage.

Years ago the accumulation of arsenic sprays (used for coddling moth control) in orchard soils increased resistance and necessitated additional spraying. The high concentration of these sprays in the fruit led Great Britain to ban importation of U.S. apples.[8] The effect of the runoff of these chemicals on our waterways and wildlife is not within the scope of this book, but is an additional concern.

Dwarf Container Varieties

Definitely begin with a dwarf variety if you will be planting your apple

---

7. USDA Pesticide Data Program, 2010.

8. Fred Lape, *Apples and Man* (New York: Van Nostrand Reinhold, 1979).

trees in containers. As fruit size is the same, even some commercial growers use dwarf varieties because they can reach fruit at the tops of the trees more easily. Dwarf trees reach 5'–7' tall and can be pruned to even smaller heights. Standard trees grow to about 35'.

Apple trees are made dwarf by grafting the desired variety onto a dwarfing "rootstock." Dwarfing rootstocks can be identified by the labels M27 or M9. Semi-dwarfing stocks, better for espaliers and bushes, are labeled M7 or M4.

Dwarf and semi-dwarf apples are often common varieties, such as Braeburn or MacIntosh, that have been grafted onto a dwarf rootstock. When selecting a dwarf apple tree, determine if the rootstock is hardy in your planting zone and whether your region averages the minimum or maximum number of chill hours required for the tree to set fruit.[9] Also look for trees with resistance to diseases and pests prevalent in your growing region.

It is said the tastiest apples were bred and grown in the United States from 1790–1900, before commercial demand for longer shelf life over-rode consumer taste preferences. Some of these heirloom varieties do still exist. Yellow Northern Spy grows in the North East, though it's susceptibility to wire worms has sidelined this delicious apple to home garden production. It is the parent tree of Jonathan and several other modern apple breeds. MacIntosh has been grown in the U.S. since the early 1900s.[10] Stayman Winesap, developed as a cross between Stayman and Winesap in 1866, appears to perform well in humid conditions. You might consider these "heirloom," or "antique" apple tree varieties since these have developed natural resistance to some diseases and usually have more fla-

Yield

A dwarf apple tree will yield 1–5 bushels (126–630 apples) per year during its peak years of production. Three to four dwarf apple trees would produce about enough to feed each in a family of four one apple per day per year (1456 apples).

Chill Hours for Apples

Apple trees do need a certain number of "chill hours" to produce apples. When selecting varieties for warmer climates, pay special attention to this requirement or your tree might not get cold enough to produce fruit. In areas that don't go below 50°F, you'll have a difficult time producing apples.

Regardless of the variety, make sure to provide protection for containerized apple trees if temperatures drop below 15°F.

---

9. For more information about chill hours, see chapter 5 about Peaches and nectarines.

10. *Apples and Man* by Fred Lape is an excellent resource on heirloom apple varieties.

vor than apples grown for commercial production.

When selecting apple trees, pay close attention to pollination requirements. Stayman-Winesap, for example cannot pollinate other trees. Note that if you are growing apple trees indoors, you will need to be the pollinator!

Finding an organic version of the apple tree you want to purchase may be difficult. I don't worry too much about buying young trees that have been grown organically because it takes 2–3 years for a tree to really begin producing fruit anyway. By the time you begin harvesting your fruit, there will be little to no chemicals available to the fruit. Just re-pot trees in organic soil and treat them organically thereafter. Your first few harvests will have far lower levels of pesticides (if any) compared to commercially grown apples and, over time, will have none.

Order trees in late winter for the greatest selection.

Planting Dates

Fruit trees are generally planted when dormant in early spring or late fall. Trees are planted in early spring in cool and moderate climates. In warm climates, they are usually planted in the fall.

If you wait until after they leaf out, you will have a difficult time purchasing trees through mail order nurseries. However, I have purchased potted, non–dormant trees in late spring at local garden centers.

Location

Wind: It's best to locate apple trees in a sunny place that is protected from constant or high winds. A windy environment can stunt the growth of apple trees. Staking the tree provides some support in windy environments.

Sunlight: Apple trees require nearly full sun for good fruit production. Morning sun is especially important for drying the moisture off leaves and preventing disease. However, I find that younger trees appreciate a little shade during our hot Florida afternoons.

Moisture

Having control of moisture is an advantage of growing apple trees in containers. As apple trees are sensitive to excess moisture, you should place your tree in an area where you can limit the amount of rain it receives.

Temperature

Containerized apple tree roots are subject to freezing if the soil temperature falls below 15°F. In cold areas, it's best to prepare for winter by insulating your container or moving it to a warmer area. To insulate a container, wrap it in an insulating material such as bubble wrap, burlap bags, or old blankets. It's also fine to move dormant apple trees to an unheated garage or basement, but you may still need to protect the roots from freezing.

Container Choice & Preparation

You will need a large, 15–20 gallon pot to give your tree adequate room for root growth. Ensure that the pot has drainage holes in the bottom

Soil

For maximum production, begin with a rich soil that has a pH in the 5.8–6.5 range. Container gardens typically become more acidic overtime. Check the pH of your soil every three years and adjust with lime as necessary to keep it in the proper range. Wood ashes and dolomite lime raise pH. Elemental sulfur is most commonly used to decrease pH. Inexpensive and fairly accurate pH meters can be purchased at most garden centers.

Planting

In a 15–20 gallon pot, place copper scrubbing pads over drainage holes. This will deter slugs and other pests from entering your pot through the holes. Add stones to cover the bottom of the pot. Gently remove your tree from its former pot or bag. Carefully untangle the main roots. If the roots are circling, cut these with pruners (it won't hurt your plant and will encourage the roots to grow straight.) Hold the plant against the outside of the pot. If the roots are too long for the pot, prune these back to fit the roots within a couple inches of the bottom. NOTE: It's best to prune roots on an angle. Place the tree in your new container and note the area at the base of the plant that is swollen. This is where the top part of the tree was grafted onto the rootstock. Hold the tree up so that this graft union is within 1" of the rim of the container. Mound soil in the pot and spread roots out over the soil. Keeping the tree at this level, add soil to just below the point of the union. Gently pat the soil around the tree, add mulch and water thoroughly.

While your tree is small, keep it staked. This becomes especially important when it begins putting on fruit. Sometimes the weight of the fruit will pull a branch over and the whole plant will come out of its container. I usually remove fruit from my trees during the first season if the weight is too heavy for the branches. To add support, use a stake or trellis, about the height of the plant. Loosely tie the stake with string or twisties. Remember to loosen the string as the tree grows.

Fertilization

Adequate phosphorous and nitrogen is critical for flowering and fruiting. Fish emulsion is a good choice for these nutrients. Dilute one tablespoon fish emulsion to one gallon of water. Apply monthly during the non-dormant season. If leaves turn yellow or pale green, increase fertilizing time to twice monthly and even weekly if necessary. Begin to reduce fertilizing at the end of summer. When you have completely stopped fertilizing by late fall, the tree will begin to go dormant for the winter.

Pests & Diseases

When gardening organically, you may see a few pests and have to endure a small amount of disfigurement to your fruit, but in general pests and disease are not too damaging to apple trees in containers. Choosing an heirloom variety that is naturally resistant to pests and disease is an excellent first step in producing healthy fruit.

A keen eye will keep pests in check. An occasional "snack" by an insect is one thing, a meal is another! Chapter 14 includes information on fighting specific pests and diseases.

Pruning

Recent studies have demonstrated that trees develop stronger trunks if the lower limbs are not pruned until the tree is one year old. Your tree will most likely already be at least one year old, so branches below the bushy head of the tree should be pruned back at the time of planting. Aggressive pruning can be avoided by training young trees before they begin to branch out extensively. Young branches can be bent and tied in the optimal growing direction. On many apple trees, fruit is produced at the tips of "spurs." Spurs are 3"–5" branches that flower and set fruit. It is important not to remove these when pruning or you may decrease fruit production. Some spurs may remain dormant for a year or more before they begin fruiting again. The

Fig. 2-1: Young apple tree

Some Apple Pests
- Coddling Moths
- Plum Curculios
- Maggots
- Mites

Some Apple Diseases
- Apple Scab
- Cedar-Apple Rust
- Powdery Mildew
- Rust
- Black Rot

main objective when pruning apple trees is to increase sunlight throughout the growing season, but it is best to save major pruning until dormancy. For successful fruit production, apple trees should form a "leader" in the center of the tree and have widely spaced limbs below the leader. Side shoots just below the main leader will form the "crown" of the apple tree. This pyramid shape allows sunlight to penetrate the lower branches. Space between the main branches allows plenty of air to circulate throughout the tree canopy.

Begin by "heading" the leader of young trees (not younger than one year) when they have reached 30″–35″ tall. Cut the leader close to a bud so as not to leave an unproductive stump at the top of the tree. Any vertical, main branches close in height to the central leader should be removed.

Next, prune off any branches growing toward the ground. Branches crisscrossing or otherwise competing with other branches should be removed. Vertical branches in close proximity to the trunk will form narrow crotches and should be removed. Be sure to leave about 6″ between branches as you move up the tree trunk. When looking at the tree from a distance, you should see space between the main branches. Horizontal branches should be longest at the bottom of the tree canopy and there should be no small branches near the trunk. Each lateral branch should fan out at the end and the entire tree should be pyramid shaped, with the tip of the tree being tallest in the center.

When the tree has reached its fruiting years, ensure good production in the lower section of the tree by "tipping" the terminal ends of the shoots just enough to allow sunlight to penetrate. Tipping should only be done during the dormant season.

> **Pruning Cuts**
>
> There are two basic types of pruning cuts for apple trees: thinning cuts and heading cuts.
>
> **Thinning Cuts**—can be used to shape your tree or remove center branches and allow more air circulation and sunlight. Cut the branch back to the point where it originates on another branch or on the trunk. To increase productivity, remove any dead or diseased limbs from the inner portion of the tree.
>
> **Heading Cuts**—removing the tip of a branch to force formation of side branches. Use this method when you want an area of your tree to bush out more. Heading cuts are made to branches emerging from the thicker portion of the trunk, closer to the ground and beneath the point where the tree branches begin to fan out. Make the cut just after a node (the point where a branch grows off) so as not to leave an unsightly stump.[1]
>
> ---
>
> 1. Clemson Extension Home & Garden Information Center, "Pruning and Growing Apple and Pear Trees HGIC 1351," http://hgic.clemson.edu.

Harvesting

The effect of harvesting on the nutritive value of apples is chief among reasons to grow your own or purchase from small, local growers. As is frequently done in large commercial operations, picking apples before they are ripe causes reduced nutritional value and flavor. Up to 50% of Vitamin C content, for example, is lost in apples when stored at temperatures above 36°F. Mechanical picking is another problem with store bought apples as it often causes extensive bruising and degradation of the fruit. Proper harvesting is critical to the nutrition and flavor of apples.[11] The Pennings Family of Pennings Orchards recommends picking apples in the following way:

"Place the palms of your hands on each apple, at the same time. Gently use your fingers—without putting too much pressure on the apples—to twist and turn the two apples either upward or downward until they release. If there is anything more than the stems on your apples after they release, then you didn't quite do it as we do. It's ok, as long as you don't drop any and don't shake off any apples from the tree."[12]

Storage

As detailed above, fresh apples are more nutritious than stored apples. If you choose to store them, however, keep them at 34°–36°F. Humidity levels should be maintained between 85%–90%. Early fruiting varieties do not usually store as well as later fruiting varieties. Apples release ethylene gas that will hasten spoilage of fruit and vegetables. Spreading out the fruit and providing adequate air circulation reduces the buildup of this gas and helps preserve your fruit. Do not store any fruit that is bruised.

Apples can also be preserved by drying, canning, freezing, and juicing.

---

11. J.I. Rodale, *How to Grow Vegetables and Fruits by The Organic Method* (Emmaus, PA: Rodale Books, 1970) 685-686.

12. Pennings Orchards, Warwick NY. www.penningsorchard.com.

Chapter 3

Revered as a member of the "holy trinity"—Celery, Carrots and Onions—in New Orleans cuisine and equally necessary with peanut butter in the diets of many youngsters, it is not surprising the average American consumed six pounds of celery in 2009. Given the challenges of growing celery in large quantities, it is also not surprising the extent of pesticides applied to this vegetable.

There are three main types of celery:

- **Cutting Celery**, also known as Celery Leaf (best kind for container gardening)
- **Traditional Stalk Celery**
- **Bulb Celery**, also known as Celeriac (grown for the underground bulb)

Since this book is designed to be

Pesticide Residue Ranking: #2

Nutritional Information[1]

Cutting Celery is said to be high in Vitamin A. It has traditionally been grown as an herb and is not included in most nutritional databases. A reliable source of nutritional information on celery leaf was not found.

Two medium stalks of celery contain about 11 calories. Stalk celery is a good source of fiber, Vitamins C, B1, and B6. It contains high levels of potassium, offsetting its high sodium content.[2] Celery is high in the phytochemicals, coumarins.

---

1. USDA National Nutrient Database for Standard Reference, Release 20 (2007).

2. J. Anderson, L. Young, and E. Long, "Potassium and Health," Colorado State University Extension—Nutrtition Resources, http://www.ext.colostate.edu/PUBS/foodnut/09355.html

a practical guide to gardening I am hesitant to recommend planting stalk celery in containers. It is a difficult plant to grow, requiring a long period of cool temperatures and a steady supply of water. Celeriac is easier to grow, but produces a very large bulb and requires more space than celery leaf or stalk celery. Cutting celery provides an alternative to growing less cooperative types. It tastes like celery, but resembles the herb parsley more than the celery we are used to purchasing at the grocery store. Cutting celery has a cut-and-come-again nature, making it an excellent choice for container gardening. Instructions for growing cutting celery follow. For the adventurous gardener, cultivation information for stalk celery is also included.

General Information

Cutting celery, or "celery leaf" (*Apium graveolens* var secalinum), is a leafy, herb-like plant. Like stalk celery, cutting celery is a biennial. Leaves of cutting celery can be harvested at any time, but the seeds are only harvested every two years. Full height is approximately 12."

Stalk celery (*Apium graveolens* var dulce) has long, thick, rigid stems. Leaves are soft in texture and light to medium green. Plant height at maturity is approximately 20."

Residue (on stalk celery)[13]

All celery samples tested positive for Chlorantraniliiprole and Spinosad. Other pesticides found on celery include include Methoxyfenozide and Permethrins.

Botanical Name

Cutting Celery
Apium graveolens
var secalinum

Stalk Celery
Apium graveolens
var dulce

Recommended Container Varieties

Cutting Celery
Afina, Zwolsche, Krul

Stalk Celery
Amsterdam, Dinant, Ventura

For additional varieties, see *Vegetable Varieties for Gardeners*, http://vegvariety.cce.cornell.edu. Cornell's College of Agriculture and Life Sciences ranks vegetables for taste, yield, ease of growing and other criteria.

Yield

One bunch of celery stalks grows approximately every 80 days. One bunch of cutting celery, comparable to a bunch of parsley, grows about every 80 days.

---

[13]. Pesticide residue information on Celery Leaf was not found.

Planting Dates

Start seeds in early spring, 2–3 months before the normal last frost date.

Container Choice & Preparation

Stalk and cutting celery are shallow rooted. For these plants, 2–5 gallon containers are adequate.

Cutting Celery

As with most plants, containers should have adequate drainage. Begin with at least three drainage holes. Add a layer of gravel or pot shards to the container before adding potting soil.

Stalk Celery

Stalk celery prefers a wet, mucky soil. Self-watering containers are excellent for maintaining moist soil. My ten year old son grew it successfully in a traditional ten gallon container with no drainage holes. The deeper container and extra moisture may have helped the plant survive a hot Florida summer.

Soil

Cutting Celery

Cutting Celery needs a light, well draining soil with a neutral to slightly acidic pH. It prefers a steady supply of minerals, including boron, calcium, magnesium, and phosphorous.

Stalk Celery

Stalk celery prefers a pH of 5.8–6.7.

Optimum Growing Conditions

- **Location/Sun Exposure:** Prefer full sun to partial shade. Steady temperatures are important for growing stalk celery. When the weather warms, move containers to a shaded area.
- **Moisture:** Cutting celery grows best when kept consistently moist, but not soggy. Stalk celery requires consistently moist soil.
- **Temperature:** Cutting Celery prefers a temperate climate, 60º–75ºF. In warmer climates, place plants in partial shade.

  Cutting celery is frost tolerant, but should be protected from freezing. Stalk celery prefers consistently cool temperatures, 60º–70ºF. It bolts quickly in warmer temperatures and dies in cold weather.

Begin with one bag of composted manure and one bag of potting soil. Thoroughly saturate soil with water. Soil should stay wet at all times.

Purchasing Seeds

Celery is propagated by seeds. Cutting celery varieties may be difficult to find locally, but are available from many online merchants.

Stalk celery seeds are usually available anywhere vegetable seeds are sold.

Growing Instructions

For cutting celery & stalk celery, plant seeds indoors 12–16 weeks before transplanting outdoors. Soak seeds overnight and then soak in warm (not hot) water for 30 minutes prior to sowing. Soaking at 118°F is said to hasten germination. Seeds can be killed in hotter temperatures, however.

> ### Pests & Diseases
>
> Cutting celery is largely unaffected by pests and diseases. It occasionally becomes a stopping place for caterpillars.
>
> Stalk celery is occasionally affected by leaf blights and celery mosaic. For prevention and treatment information, see chapter 14.

Celery seeds are tiny and difficult to handle. Some gardeners mix the seeds with a small amount of white sand so they can see where seeds have been planted. Moisten soil thoroughly before sowing. Sprinkle the seeds/sand evenly in a tray of soil. Press seeds into the top of soil and then spread a very thin layer of sand over the tiny seeds. Always bottom water celery seedlings to prevent damping off disease. To bottom water, place a tray without drainage holes beneath your tray of soil. Add water to the bottom tray. Soil in the top tray will absorb water from the bottom tray, keeping the soil, not the plants, consistently wet. Self watering containers have built in water reservoirs designed to bottom water plants. These can be purchased online or at home improvement stores. Maintain temperatures around 60°–75°F.

A few days prior to transplanting, reduce the amount of water you give them. They may wilt slightly. This practice is thought to reduce bolting when moving celery plants to colder outside temperatures. Space seedlings 6" apart. Mulch the plants with grass clippings or straw.

Fertilization

Fertilize with fish emulsion monthly.

Harvesting

Cutting Celery

Cut within 2" of its base. It may

Fig. 3-1: Celery plant. *Celery is one of the few garden plants that thrives in wet soil.*

be harvested every 8–10 weeks until its second year, when it will produce seeds and then die.

Stalk Celery

Cut stalk celery at maturity with a sharp knife just below soil level.

Use/Storage

Cutting Celery

For fresh use, place stalks in a jar of water and refrigerate 3–5 days. To use celery leaf as an herb, try dehydrating on a drying rack or in a food dehydrator. Minced celery leaf frozen in ice cubes make flavorful additions to soup stocks.

Stalk Celery

Rinse with water and dry thoroughly. For longer shelf life, cover with aluminum foil and store in refrigerator for up to two weeks.

Chapter 4

STRAWBERRIES, MOTHER NATURE'S CANDY

Of all the fruits and veggies included in the Dirty Dozen, I was most shocked when I discovered strawberries were high on the list. Strawberries! Full of nutrients, easy to eat, wonderful flavor...how could strawberries have any evil lurking in them? So attractive and delicious, strawberries were the one food I was always able to get my boys to eat when they were toddlers.

Now I know better and I try to do the right thing. I either buy organic strawberries or grow my own. The trouble with store bought organic strawberries is the price, quality, and availability. At over $4 a pound, we can't really

> **Pesticide Residue Ranking: #3**

> **Nutritional Information**
>
> In addition to having high levels of cancer fighting phytochemicals, strawberries are a great source of Vitamin C. At 89.4 mg, one cup (152 g) of strawberries contains about 20 mg more than the USDA Daily Recommended Values for the average person. In this one cup of strawberries, you'll also consume about 3 g of fiber, 24 mg of calcium, and 49 calories.
>
> USDA National Nutrient Database for Standard Reference, Release 20 (2007).

afford to snack on store bought organic strawberries each time we pass through the kitchen. Unfortunately, the quality of store bought strawberries is also an issue. They rot quickly and tend to grow lovely white lab coats after just one or two days in the refrigerator. They are also very seasonal. Quality strawberries are only available in our local grocery store in late summer and early fall. Is it possible to grow your own strawberries organically and have a better supply? Absolutely. In fact, it's easy.

General Information

Strawberry plants are self pollinating herbaceous perennials. The plants average 8" tall and 9" spread. Strawberry plants are propagated by seeds, division, and tissue culture. There are four basic types of strawberry plants:

- June Bearing
- Ever Bearing
- Day Neutral
- Alpine

June bearing strawberries produce one large crop each summer. Ever bearing strawberries produce 2–3 smaller crops in summer and early fall. Day Neutral and alpine varieties fruit repeatedly throughout the summer and early fall.

Residue

Captan, Pyroclostrabin, Boscalid and THPI were found most frequently on strawberries samples. Thirty nine different pesticides were found on strawberries sampled by the USDA. Thirteen different pesticides were found on a single sample. The average number of pesticides found in all samples was 1.47.

June Bearing Varieties

June bearing varieties are reliable producers and, as all fruit ripens at once, will provide enough fruit at one time for fresh eating, freezing, baking, and even sharing. In mild climates, June bearing strawberry varieties often act like ever bearing varieties, producing smaller quantities throughout the summer instead of one large crop in June. June bearing crops usually do not produce a large crop until the second growing season.

Day Neutral Varieties

These varieties are are good in con-

Botanical Name

Family: *Rosaceae*

Fragaria x ananassa
(June Bearing, Ever Bearing & Day Neutral)

Fragaria vesca (Alpine)

Yield

An average strawberry plant produces 1 quart of strawberries per year. Just a few pots can keep you in strawberries for much of the year.

tainers as they do not produce many runners. They are preferred for their steady supply of fruit through most of the growing season. These varieties are a little more fickle than the others, however.

Alpine Varieties

This type produces smaller fruit than other strawberry varieties, but their flavor is candy sweet. If you prefer flavor over quantity, I highly recommend these little gems from Europe.

Health benefits of specific strawberry varieties: A recent Cornell study indicates that some strawberry varieties have higher cancer fighting properties than others. Earliglow scored the highest with a 65% difference between Earliglow and lowest ranked (Allstar) variety that was tested.[14]

Planting Dates

Seeds: Sow seeds thirty days before you intend to transplant.

Plants: Order plants early and request shipping at the optimal planting time for your growing zone. This will ensure the nursery does not run out before you get a chance to order. Gardeners in most regions plant their strawberries in early spring after the last freeze. In warmer regions, USDA plant hardiness zones 7–10, plant in the fall.

---

14. Katherine J. Meyers, Christopher B. Watkins, Marvin P. Pritts, and Rui Hai Liu, "Antioxidant and Antiproliferative Activities of Strawberries," Department of Food Science, Department of Horticulture, and Institute of Comparative and Environmental Toxicology, Cornell University (August, 2003).

Recommended June Bearing Varieties

- **Earliglow**—Excellent Flavor and Texture. Wilt Resistant.
- **Camarosa**—High yield. Good flavor.
- **Lateglow**—Excellent Flavor and Texture. Wilt Resistant.

Recommended Day Neutral Varieties

Tristar & Tribute—Tristar peaks earlier than Tribute so plant both these varieties for a steady harvest. Produces medium to small fruit. Excellent choices for dessert quality fruit. Good wilt resistance.

Recommended Alpine Variety

I prefer **Alexandria**. Alpine varieties grow well in partial shade and in cool weather.

Recommended Everbearing Varieties

- **Quinalt**—Ready to harvest just 4–5 weeks after planting. Very tasty.
- **Albion Organic**—Crowns available from a few mail order catalogs. Good disease resistance.

Fig. 4-1: Planting a terra-cotta strawberry pot

Location

Place strawberry pots in full sun in an area protected from excess moisture. Alpine strawberry plants prefer partial shade.

Bring plants indoors before a freeze. In milder climates, plants can stay outside, but mulch to maintain consistent root temperatures.

Container Choice

There are a lot of fun container options for strawberries. Hanging planters, terra-cotta "strawberry pots" with the pockets built into the sides, and conventional pots are all adequate for growing strawberries. I prefer hanging plastic baskets with a water reservoir. They require less planting time, rarely dry out, and are attractive.

Adequate drainage is essential when growing strawberries. The container should have at least two drainage holes in the bottom or sides. Cover the bottom of the pot with at least ¼" drainage material.

Fig. 4-2: Hanging strawberry plants

Fig. 4-3: Pot with water reservoir

If you select a deep pot, such as the terra cotta strawberry pot, a central drainage core should also be inserted (see Fig. 4-1). Using a 2" pvc pipe about 4" shorter than the container, drill holes every 2"–3" along the pipe. This is not easy! Place the pipe in a vice before you begin to keep it from spinning while you drill. Follow all standard safety precautions when using the drill. Bury the bottom of the tube in the drainage gravel in your container. The tube will become more stable as you add plants and soil. Then add soil to about 1" below the first pocket in the strawberry pot. Insert a crown from the inside, gently feeding the top of the crown through the pocket to the pot's exterior. The roots should point toward the bottom of the pot and should not crimp or form a "J." It takes a little practice, but you'll soon be accurately estimating how much soil to add to the next level while still allowing space for the roots. The root end of the crown should sit just inside the outer edge of the pocket. Gently add soil to cover the roots. Pat the soil lightly and add additional soil to repeat the process for the next level of pockets.

Barrel Method

If you are lucky enough to have half a wooden barrel, it will serve nicely as a planter. Consider adding casters to the bottom of the barrel to make moving it easier. Begin by drilling several holes in the bottom for drainage. Then, beginning about 8" from the bottom of the barrel, drill holes 3" in diameter, 12" apart around the barrel. Continue to drill holes around the barrel, leaving about 8" between rows and staggering the holes as you go up. As with the strawberry pot, add a central drainage pipe to the barrel. The pipe should have several small holes along the length of

---

Optimum Growing Conditions

- **Location/Sun Exposure:** Place strawberry pots in full sun in an area protected from excess moisture. Alpine strawberry plants prefer partial shade.

- **Moisture:** Strawberry plants generally prefer about 1" of water a week. Keep soil consistently moist until fruits begin to mature. When fruits begin to ripen, allow the soil to dry between waterings and avoid getting water directly on fruit. High humidity can create fungus problems in strawberries. Conserve moisture and prevent fungus and mold growth on fruit by placing straw between the fruit and soil. Once every two weeks, remove the saucer from beneath your pot and water the soil thoroughly. Allowing the water to run through will leach much of the sodium that builds up in container garden soil.

- **Temperature:** For germination, strawberry plants require cool night time temperatures (50°–60°F) and moderate day temperatures (60°–70°F). Most strawberry plants grow best in cool temperatures, 65°–75°F, however our June bearing varieties are still thriving and bearing fruit in mid July. Gardeners in hot climates can provide light shade to extend the growing season.

the pipe for even water distribution.

Add soil and plants to the barrel in the same way described for the terra cotta strawberry pot, above. Gently spread out the roots and add soil to the next level of holes. Continue adding soil and placing the plants in the holes until you have reached the top. Add a few strawberry plants to the center of the barrel, with adequate soil between the plants and the pipe. Add water and fertilizer to the barrel through the pipe.

Planting Procedure

Seeds

Begin by refrigerating your seed for 24 hours. Prepare the planting medium (see soil recipe on the next page) in a flat tray and moisten it evenly. Now sprinkle strawberry seeds uniformly across the medium. Don't worry about counting the seeds and spacing them. It's too much work! You can always thin them out later if necessary. Cover with a very thin layer of soil or vermiculite (they require some light for germination so don't cover with a thick layer of soil).

Strawberries prefer cool germination temperatures (50°–60°F at nights and 60°–70°F in the day), but need full sun to germinate.

In 2–4 weeks, you will begin to see sprouts. Your long awaited babies will continue to grow for you if you place them in full sun. Keep the soil evenly moist, but not saturated. Provide plenty of air circulation. When your seedlings

Fig. 4-4: Flat under fluorescent light. *Two of these flats, available at garden stores, fit under a standard shop light hung above plants. Plastic domes are available for keeping seeds moist before they sprout. The light should be kept about 4"–5" above the tallest plants. A light is useful for young seedlings like Celery, Lettuce, Peppers, Tomatoes, & Strawberries from seed, especially when window space is scarce.*

have two sets of leaves, transplant to 3" peat pots and continue to baby them. In three to four weeks, once plants are bushy and well established, remove the bottoms from the peat pots and plant them, pots and all, into containers. The top of the peat pots should be at the same level as the top of the soil in your container.

Crowns: See "Container Choice" above.

Propagation from Division & Runners

Division: This method is easier than starting from seed. Use it to replenish your garden stock at least every 2–3 years. Day Neutral and Alpine varieties have few runners so you will need to divide the crowns with a sharp knife. This is not a difficult procedure. Just make sure that each section you divide has roots and leaves. Slice through the section and plant in fresh soil.

Transplanting Runners: June bearing varieties have runners that can be cut off from the mother plant and replanted. Varieties that produce many runners are not usually considered the best varieties for container growth, but any runners that have rooted can be used for propagation.

Soil

Strawberries love rich, well-draining soil with a pH range of 5.5–6.5. The quick and easy method of selecting soil is to buy a bag of organic potting soil from your local garden center. It will have adequate nutrients and texture and you will most likely be able to grow a satisfactory crop of strawberries with minimal work and expense.

If you want to maximize your yield and be absolutely sure your soil is ideal for growing strawberries, I recommend the recipe and instructions listed below.

Soil Recipe for Strawberries

- 1 Part Potting Soil
- 1 Part Composted Manure (may be purchased in bags at garden centers)
- 1 Part Peat Moss
- 1 Part Perlite
- 1 Part Vermiculite

All of these ingredients can be purchased at your local garden center. Mix the first four ingredients together and dampen with diluted fish emulsion or kelp water.

Soil pH for Container Gardens

I rarely check the pH in my container gardens when I first plant. Potting soil is usually balanced pretty well. pH and nutrient levels in containers do change over time, however, so testing and amending throughout the growing season may reward you with higher yields.

Strawberries prefer a pH of 5.6–6.2. Using litmus paper or a pH testing kit, check the pH and adjust your soil with limestone to raise pH (½ TB per 2 ½ gallon pot.) For alkaline soil, add ½ pint of cider vinegar per 2 ½ gallon plant container.

Fertilization

Feed plants when blossoms appear, again when buds appear, and after the harvest. Kelp or fish emulsion are good choices for feeding strawberries.

Pests & Diseases[15]

Birds: How do so many birds know to visit my garden when the strawberries are beginning to ripen? I'm beginning to think they watch the plants as closely as I do and make daily checks to see if the fruit has ripened yet. I recommend covering plants with garden netting. This can be purchased at garden centers or online and can be cut to the size of your container.

Diseases: Careful selection of varieties, good soil, and frequent inspection of plants will reduce most strawberry diseases. Wet weather can be a cause of increased fungus growth. In this situation, a commercial grower would need to prevent disease by spraying acres of crops with fungicides. Container gardeners can move their strawberries to a more protected location and save the crop without extensive use of chemicals.

See Chapter 14 for identification, prevention and treatment information.

Harvesting & Storage

Strawberries are fully ripe when uniformly red. Pick the berries with the caps and stems attached to retain firmness and quality. Pinch the stem off about ¼" above the cap. Don't pull them off. Strawberries should be picked about every other day in warm weather, every 3–4 days in cool weather. The harvest period for some June-bearing varieties may last three to four weeks. Strawberries can be stored in the refrigerator for up to 5–7 days. Optimum storage conditions are a temperature of 32°F and a relative humidity of 90%–95%.

When harvesting small fruits, pick and the handle carefully. Rough treatment will damage fruit, reducing its storage life and leading to greater spoilage.

It is best to pick strawberries early in the coolest part of the day. Pick berries when they are uniformly red. Once fruit begins to ripen, watch closely and plan to harvest every day or two. Pinch or clip stems about ¼" above the cap of the strawberry. Strawberries will last longer if some of the stem and the cap

---

Some Strawberry Pests
- Slugs, Snails
- Birds
- Tarnished Plant Bugs

Some Strawberry Diseases
- Mold
- Fungus

---

15. cf. Barbara W. Ellis and Fen Marshall Bradley, The Organic Gardener's Handbook of Natural Insect and Disease Control, (Emmaus, PA: Rodale Press, 1992) 216-220.

are left attached. Handle fruit gently to prevent bruising. Strawberries keep 3–4 days in the refrigerator. If you have planted several strawberry plants, plan ahead to store the excess harvest. Strawberries can be frozen or made into preserves.

Source for More Information

The Garden Primer by Barbara Damrosch (Workman Publishing, 1988) 382–387.

Chapter 5

PEACHES & NECTARINES

The flavor of a fresh picked peach is a memorable experience. As a child, I used to eat peaches off the tree while visiting family in Georgia. Even more than the other fruits on the Dirty Dozen list, a peach from your own tree will truly reward you with flavor you cannot buy in the grocery store.

I include peaches and nectarines in the same chapter because nectarines are a smooth skinned, slight genetic variation of peaches. Growing information is the same for both fruits.

Peach trees are deciduous, so they drop their leaves every autumn. They enter dormancy in late fall and flower in early spring. Leaves are bright green, usually 3"–5" long. Bark on a peach tree is smooth and brown.

Pesticide Residue Ranking

Peaches: #4
Nectarines: #6
(imported nectarines)

Nutritional Information

60 calories in 1 cup (raw). Peaches and Nectarines are good sources of potassium and vitamins A and C; low sodium; no saturated fat.

USDA National Nutrient Database for Standard Reference, Release 20 (2007).

There are two basic types of peaches—clingstone and freestone. Fruit on clingstone varieties adhere to the pit. This type of peach is often used for canning and freezing. The fruit on freestone varieties falls away from the pit. This type of peach is more often used for fresh eating.

Residue

According to the Environmental Working Group, "every sample of imported peaches tested positive for pesticide residue... As a category, peaches have been treated with more pesticides than any other produce, registering combinations of up to 57 different chemicals." Most commonly, Carbaryl, o-Phenylphenol and Cyprodinil were found on peaches. Formetanate hydrochloride, Fludioxonil, Phosmet and Iprodione residues were detected most commonly on nectarines.

Botanical Name

Peach: *Prunus persica* var. *persica*

Nectarine: *Prunus persica* var. *nucipersica*

Yield

A mature dwarf peach or nectarine tree produces about three bushels of fruit a year.

Dwarf Container Varieties

Careful selection of a variety appropriate for your growing environment will increase your chances of successfully growing peaches. An all inclusive selection of dwarf and semi-dwarf peach and nectarine trees available for each growing region would be a book in itself. I have listed a few on the following page, but recommend you contact your local cooperative extension office for cultivar recommendations specific to your growing climate. Most peach and nectarine trees are self-fertile, though a second tree will slightly increase yields. See the section on temperature for an explanation of chill hours.

Container gardening enables home gardeners in the coldest regions (USDA plant hardiness zone 5 or colder) to grow peach and nectarine trees despite an environment normally deemed too cold for these trees. See the "location" section in this chapter for tips on growing trees in cold areas.

Planting Dates

Plant peach trees in late winter when they are still dormant (buds are still closed). In very cold regions, plant in early spring—after the coldest part of the winter but when trees are still dormant. Newly planted trees should be protected from extreme cold. Trees planted in containers may be stored in a garage or basement during a late cold snap.

Recommended Peach Varieties

Region	USDA Grow Zones	Chill Hours	Variety
North East*	4–6	850 (Cresthaven) 1000 (Reliance)	Cresthaven, Reliance
Mid-Atlantic	7–8	850 (Clayton) 950 (Elberta)	Clayton, Elberta
Southeast	8–9	150 (FlordaGlo) 250 (Bonanza)	FlordaGlo, Bonanza
Upper Midwest*	2–6	850 (Elberta) 1000 (Reliance)	Reliance, Elberta
Midwest*	4–6	900–1000	Reliance, Biscoe
Southwest	7–9	450 (Rio Grande) 650 (TexStar)	Rio Grande, TexStar
Pacific Northwest*	5–6	850	Sweethaven, Harbelle
Pacific West Coast	7–9	250 (Bonanza) 500 (Honey Babe)	Bonanza, Honey Babe Miniature

Recommended Nectarine Varieties

Region	USDA Grow Zones	Chill Hours	Variety
North East*	4–6	400–500	Goldmine, Sunbonnet
Mid-Atlantic	7–8	850	Sunglo
Southeast	8–9	250 (SunMist) 275 (UFQueen)	SunMist, UFQueen
Upper Midwest*	2–6	850	Sunglo
Midwest*	4–6	800 (Mericrest) 850 (Sunglo)	Mericrest, Sunglo
Southwest	7–9	850	Crimson Gold, Red Globe
Pacific Northwest*	5–6	850	Redgold, Fantasia
Pacific West Coast	7–9	500	Fantasia, Garden Delight Miniature

*In USDA zone 5 and colder, move trees to an unheated garage or basement in winter and early spring. This will save them from damage in severe winters. The space needs to be unheated because temperatures above 45°F will not produce the necessary chill hours.

Location

Peaches prefer full sun and moderate wind protection. In areas with high humidity and frequent rain fall, choose a protected location. Container gardeners have the opportunity to grow trees outside their established growing zones. If growing peach or nectarine trees in USDA plant hardiness zones 1–5, move trees to a cold basement or garage protected from hard freezes during the winter. In the spring, trees can be placed in micro-climates such as the south side of a building to protect them from north and west winds while maximizing sun exposure. Here lies an advantage of small home gardening over large commercial operations.

Watering

Water thoroughly and then allow soil to dry between watering sessions. In average weather conditions, plants need 1" of water per week (per plant).

Temperature

Peach tree varieties are available for USDA plant hardiness zones 4–9. Peach and nectarine tree varieties require "chill hours," temperatures between 33°F–45°F. High chill varieties must receive a minimum of 600 chill hours. Moderate chill varieties must receive about 400–600 chill hours. Low chill varieties require 100–400 chill hours. Insufficient chill hour exposure will weaken trees and lower yields.

The Chart on the previous page recommends varieties for various grow zones.

Container Choice & Preparation

For 1–3 year old trees, 10–15 gallon pots are ideal. Adequate drainage is essential to successful peach and nectarine tree growth. Containers should have 2–3 drainage holes in the bottom or lower sides. Add at least 2" of gravel or pot shards in the bottom of the container.

Frost Protection & Chill Hours

When peach tree blossoms begin to open, they are susceptible to late frosts. Low chill varieties will put on blossoms earlier than high chill trees.

Planting a low chill variety in a cold climate could lead to premature blossoming during a winter warm spell. On the other hand, high chill trees planted in warmer climates may not get enough chill hours. In this case, they may not emerge properly from dormancy. Therefore, it is important to select a tree appropriate for the amount of cool temperatures in your region. See the "Recommended Peach Varieties" chart on the previous page for varieties recommended in each chill zone.

When there is a late freeze, it is important to protect peach tree blossoms. Cover trees with a semi-permeable "floating" fabric (available at most garden supply stores) or bring trees inside until the weather warms.

Purchasing Peach & Nectarine Trees

It is much easier to purchase a young tree than to start from seed or cuttings. A few companies even sell organically grown trees, though supplies are usually limited. There are a few genetically dwarf peach trees, but most varieties will not be dwarf unless they are grafted onto a dwarfing rootstock. Grafting is a fairly complicated process and beyond the scope of this book. Many agriculture extension offices provide information and classes about grafting.

Purchase dormant peach and nectarine trees on dwarf or semi-dwarf rootstock near the end of winter. One year trees are less expensive than the more established 2–3 year old trees. Three year old trees will yield fruit within the first year of your purchase. To create sturdier trees, some nurseries cut back their trees the first year and sell them the following year as one year trees on two year rootstocks. The more developed the root ball, the better, so it is worth asking about this at the time of purchase. St. Julien A (prunus institia) is generally regarded as the most compatible rootstock with peaches. P30-135 is compatible with peaches and nectarines. Growers in the southeast who intend to plant their peach trees in the ground should choose a nematode resistant rootstock, such as Flordagard.

Planting

Have soil and containers ready when plants arrive. Carefully unwrap tree and check for disease or pests. Do not keep diseased or pest infested trees. Quality trees are more likely to produce quality fruit. Examine the roots before planting. If roots are circling or matted, run a sharp knife down the sides of the area and gently tease apart the roots. Cutting the matted roots will not damage the tree and will free up the healthy roots.

> **Potting Soil for Peaches & Nectarines**
>
> Commercial organic fruit soil mixtures are readily available at local and internet garden centers. To maximize production, use the mix below. Soil pH should be about 6.5.
>
> - 2 cubic feet dampened peat moss or rotted pine bark
> - 1 cubic foot sand (washed sand or horticultural sand is fine)
> - 1 cubic foot perlite
> - 1 cubic foot organic compost
> - ½ pound dolomite lime

Place the tree in a container with gravel for drainage as outlined in "container choice and preparation" above. Add soil to bottom third of container, forming a cone of soil in the center of the container. Gently spread roots in all directions. Drape roots down each side of the soil cone, being careful not to bend or fold them. Add soil, lightly pressing to remove air pockets. Add soil up to 1" below the bud union. The bud union is the place where the tree was grafted and is evidenced by a swelling on the lower trunk (see Fig. 5-1 below).

Water tree thoroughly and place in protected area until it begins to leaf out in the spring. Water lightly once every two weeks while tree is dormant. When the weather warms, move tree to full sun and follow instructions for fertilization and watering.

Fig. 5-1: Bud union. *The bulge where the desired variety was grafted to the rootstock—also known as the "graft union." The bud union must not be buried.*

Fertilization

Fish emulsion or kelp—Two tablespoons to a gallon of water. Add to soil every two months. A soil analysis twice yearly is a good idea as peach trees need to maintain adequate nitrogen and proper pH levels for maximum fruit production and for general tree health. Do not fertilize in late summer as excess nitrogen during this time may delay dormancy.

> **Pests**
> - Oriental Fruit Moth
> - Green Peach Aphid
> - Plum Curculio
> - Tarnished Plant Bug
> - Stink Bug
> - Green Stink Bug
> - Brown Stink Bug
> - Dusky Stink Bug
> - False Chinch Bug
> - Japanese Beetle
> - Green June Beetle
> - Western Flower Thrips
> - Tufted Apple Bud Moth
> - Deer & Squirrels

Pests & Diseases

When inter-planted with peach trees, garlic and horseradish are said to ward off disease and pests. Peach and nectarine trees are highly susceptible to moisture related diseases such as mildew. Careful placement of your plants in an area where rainfall can be regulated will prevent or limit the spread of most of diseases. Though less so for trees grown in containers, peach and nectarine trees are most often affected by the pests and disease listed above on this page.

Chapter 14 includes information on fighting specific pests and diseases.

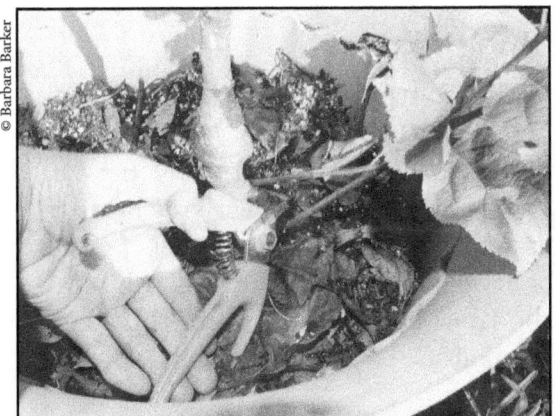

Fig. 5-2: Pruning shoots below graft union.
These shoots must be removed because they will have characteristics of the rootstock rather than the desired grafted variety of fruit tree.

Fig. 5-3: Pruning vertical shoots.
Removing vertical shoots near the trunk will allow better ventilation and penetration of sunlight.

Diseases
- Anthracnose
- Bacterial Spot
- Brown Rot
- Usicoccum Canker
- Leaf Curl
- Leucostoma Canker
- Plum Pox Virus (PPV)
- Powdery Mildew
- Prunus Stem Pitting Virus
- Rhizopus Fruit Rot
- Scab
- Verticulum Wilt
- X-Disease
- Yellows

Pruning

To reduce risk of canker and peach tree borer, it is important not to cut branches flush with the trunk or leader branch. Instead, cut back to just outside the "collar," the area of thickened bark (a ridge of wrinkled wood) where the smaller branch joins the larger limb at the base of the branch. The collar will heal the area where the cut was made. It is important not to cut the collar or to leave a long stub outside the collar.[16]

Trees less than one year should not be pruned unless shoots appear below the graft (see Fig. 5-2 above). Creating space within the canopy for ventilation and sunlight is the main goal when thinning branches. Peach trees require a light touch when pruning. Over zealous pruning will lead to decreased fruit production. Winter pruning often results in the death of peach trees.

After the first growing season, in early spring, prune peach trees to 30″ tall. Leave only three or four lateral branches growing on a 45°–55° angle to the trunk (see Fig. 5-4). Ideally, limbs

---

16. cf. Louisiana State Ag Center. www.lsuagcenter.com

should be no lower than 1 ½′ from the bottom of the trunk. The following spring, remove broken and low growing limbs. Remove any large vertical shoots growing on the inside of the tree (see Fig. 5-3). These create too much shade and decrease ventilation within the tree. Maximum fruit production occurs on branches of about 18″–24″ in length and the diameter of a pencil. Lateral branches longer than 2′ should be cut back to about 18.″

Thinning Fruit

Peach trees often overproduce fruit. If some of the fruit is not removed from the tree, the entire crop will consist of very small, hard peaches. Tree branches will often break under the weight of excess fruit. About one month after the tree reaches full bloom, thin fruit to about 6″ between peaches.

Harvest

Peaches ripen in late summer and early fall. The fruit is ready to be picked when the green tinge disappears, but the fruit is still slightly firm. Handle fruit gently and use clean harvest buckets to reduce bruising and early spoilage. Refrigerated, ripe peaches last 3–5 days. Excess can be frozen or canned for a shelf life of about 12 months. 1 ½ pounds of fresh fruit yields about one pint of frozen or canned peaches.

Fig. 5-4: Young peach tree. *Pruned to central leader.*

Fig. 5-5: Peach tree with fruit. *A month after full bloom, fruit should be thinned to 6″ apart.*

Chapter 11

SPINACH

Though they do not care for Pop-Eye's version (canned), my children love fresh spinach. My youngest son will not touch lettuce, but he is happy to munch on a bowl of spinach, stems and all.

Recent food scares about spinach underscore the advantages of growing your family's own produce. The ecoli outbreak in 2006 devastated many spinach farmers (organic and traditional.) It also scared and sickened many consumers. The Food and Drug Administration recalled all spinach while they struggled to find the source of contamination. Tracing the origins of the outbreak was nearly impossible because huge distribution operations had bought their spinach from many different sources.

In addition to having fewer pesticide residues and fresher produce, food contamination is rarely experienced by

Pesticide Residue Ranking: #11

Nutritional Information

With just 7 calories per cup (30 g) of fresh spinach, you will gain:

- 30 mg of Calcium
- 24 mg of Magnesium
- 167 mg of Potassium
- 58 mcg of Folate
- 2,813 IU of Vitamin A
- 144.9 mcg of Vitamin K

Spinach is also high in Iron, Vitamin B2, beta Carotene, Lutein, and Zeaxanthin.

Botanical Name

Spinacea oleracia

Family: *Chebioiduaceae*

those who consume the food they grow in a home garden.

Just to be safe, I have included safe produce handling tips at the end of this chapter.

General Information[17]

Spinach is a self and wind pollinating annual. Spinach ranges from 6"–12" tall and spreads 6"–12" wide. During the growing season, two 6"x6"x6" containers grown successively (every two weeks) should yield about the equivalent of one 5 oz. bag of store bought spinach each week.

Residue

Spinach ranked fifth on the Environmental Working Group's list of the Dirty Dozen. Forty eight different pesticides were detected on spinach samples tested by the USDA. Unlike many other vegetables, comparable residue quantities were found on processed spinach as well as fresh. Permethrins and Imidicloprid were detected most commonly.

Variety Selection

- Melody (My favorite for flavor)
- Viroflay (Easy to grow)

Planting Dates

Spinach is a cool weather crop. Site selection and judicious selection of cultivars can extend the season by 1–2 months. Plant to harvest time is 45–60 days, depending on the variety. Spinach needs about six weeks of temperatures below 75°F. It grows best in a temperature range of 45°–65°F.

Indoor container gardeners can grow spinach year round.

For outdoor container gardening, aim for those times of year when temperatures range from a little below freezing to about 75°F. In most regions, this means outdoor direct seeding should be done in early spring or early fall. Extend the harvest season further into the summer by succession sowing every two weeks, placing containers in partial shade, and by planting heat tolerant varieties.

Another way to extend the outdoor harvest season is to sow seeds indoors,

> ### Spinach Substitutes for Warm Weather
>
> - **New Zealand Spinach** (*Basella alba*)
> - **Malabar Spinach** (*Tetragonia tetragonioides*)
> - Japanese Spinach varieties, such as Komatsuna and Okame.
>
> These vining greens are not true spinaches, but are good for eating fresh or cooked. They thrive when temperatures are too warm for true spinach.

---

17. General spinach reference: Barbara Damrosch, *The Garden Primer*, (New York: Workman Publishing, 1988).

and later move seedlings outdoors. This gives them a head-start. For a spring crop using this method, start seedlings indoors 5–6 weeks before the usual last frost date in spring. Transplant to the outdoors or move containers outdoors after danger of freezing temperatures is past. Light frost will not harm spinach. For an outdoor fall crop, sow seeds indoors 5–6 weeks before temperatures are expected to generally remain below 75°F outside. Move plants outdoors when the cooler weather arrives.

Container Choice

Containers should be at least 6″ deep and 6″ wide. If you want to grow large quantities of spinach, consider using a half barrel. Containers should have at least three drainage holes. Add a thin layer of gravel to the bottom of the container before adding soil.

Planting Procedure

Moisten soil and sow seeds closely, about ½″ deep. Keep soil moist, not wet, until seeds germinate. When seedlings germinate, water to maintain even soil moisture, but avoid getting water directly on plants. Thin to 4″ apart when seedlings are 1″ tall. If moving the containers outside, wait until last frost and gradually introduce the plants to outdoor temperatures by leaving them outside for longer periods each day until, after 3–5 days, the plants are staying outside all day.

Thin again to 4″ apart when seedlings are 6″ tall. Enjoy the thinnings. Baby spinach tastes better than mature spinach!

Spinach likes a steady source of moisture, but it doesn't like "wet feet." Once seedlings are established, I water once daily if it is windy or warm and once every other day in cool weather.

Half way through the growing season (about 20 days), I give spinach an-

Fig. 6-1: Container spinach garden

Optimum Growing Conditions

- **Location/Sun Exposure:** Spinach prefers partial shade to full sun (depending on temperatures and climate). Protect plants from drying winds.
- **Moisture:** One inch per week (consistent moisture is critical)
- **Temperature:** Cool to cold. Mulch to maintain consistent root temperatures in winter.

other drink of fish emulsion or kelp.

Mistakes & Troubleshooting

Spinach will go to flower early when temperatures stay about 75°F for long periods of time. Plant covers and mulch can delay bolting. Warmer climate gardeners will have a longer growing period if they use heat resistant cultivars, such as New Zealand, or wait until late fall to plant their spinach.

To avoid disturbing the roots, I usually like to start plants in peat pots. I had limited results with this method when I planted spinach, however. Spinach tends to push its roots back to the surface. As a result, the peat pots kept rising up in the soil and toppling over. To solve the problem, I uprighted the spinach pots and packed soil around them. They finally developed enough of a root system to stay upright. Then they grew beautifully, but I think that it took a little longer than it would have if I had just planted them straight into the containers.

For my second batch, I scattered spinach seeds straight into a 12" wide by 14" deep container. I left the tub outside on my pool deck and watered every day. The seeds sprouted promptly, but struggled to grow due to shading caused by the edge of the tall pot. I moved the pot away from a northern wall so that it could receive full overhead sun and the seedlings began to grow more vigorously.

Some Spinach Pests
- Caterpillars
- Leaf miners
- Flea Beetles

Some Spinach Diseases
- Fusarium wilt
- Mildew
- Anthracnose
- Nitrogen deficiency

For prevention & treatment information, see Chapter 14.

Soil Recipe for Spinach
- 2 Parts Organic Potting Soil
- 1 part peat moss
- 1 part perlite
- 1 part vermiculite
- 2 Tb Fish Emulsion in 1 gallon of water (mix in enough of this Feeding Water to thoroughly moisten the soil)

Spinach is a heavy feeder. I like to spray my containers of soil with diluted fish emulsion or kelp a day or two before planting.

Harvesting & Storage

In just a month and a half, your spinach will be ready to harvest. In cool temperatures, the harvesting period should last about a month. Using scissors, snip the outside leaves of the spinach. When the outer leaves have started to grow back, snip the inner leaves. It's time to cut the whole plant when you see buds forming in the center of the plant. Hopefully, you've already started another pot of spinach so the end of your first crop won't create too great a sense of loss (You laugh now, but just wait).

Refrigerated, spinach should last about one week. If blanched first, spinach will last months in the freezer.

Extending the Season

Judicious use of cold frames in the winter and switching varieties as the weather warms can extend the growing season to six months. Here's how I do it in North Florida:

- **September:**
  I plant New Zealand and Malabar Spinach in pots outside.

- **October/November:**
  I plant Melody in pots outside.

- **December:**
  I plant Melody in pots and cover with a light row cover. When plants are 2" tall, I mulch with straw. If we have an early freeze, I bring the pots onto my patio at night.

- **January/February:**
  I plant Melody in pots and place them in a small cold frame.

- **March/April/May:**
  Depending on temperatures, I plant either Melody or New Zealand/Malabar in pots outside.

Arugula

Though it is not on the Dirty Dozen list, I also grow Arugula throughout the winter season. I like the combination of its peppery taste with the mellow flavor of spinach in salads.

Get the Kids Involved!

When kids plant and care for spinach and other veggies, they also tend to at least try eating it.

Safe Handling of Produce from the Garden

1. Whenever handling food, you should first wash your hands. This includes food in the garden. It's quite possible to transfer germs from your home to your produce. After working in the garden, you should again wash your hands.

2. Wash all produce when you bring it into your home. I admit that my family often eats unwashed produce right off the plant, but I don't recommend this practice.

3. Prevent your pets from using your container garden for a bathroom. Covering the soil with mulch is usually an adequate deterrent. I have had a few persistent cats that don't mind scratching away the mulch, so I also add decorative rock to my containers. If this doesn't work, I place wooden shisk-a-bob sticks, pointy sides up, in my pots. That always does the trick.

4. After the harvest, clean containers with diluted bleach. This will kill most pathogens that might be passed on to your next crop.

5. Be careful when using composted manure in your garden. It is essential that the pile eat up to 105°–145°F to kill pathogens. I am not aware of any cases where gardens were contaminated from the use of composted manure, but it makes sense to monitor the temperature.

6. Always use new potting soil when planting a new crop. I throw the old soil out on my lawn.

Chapter 7

GRAPES

Muscadine grapes can be found growing wild in North and Central Florida. Discovering the large, sweet fruit growing wild on a fence line or arbor is always a delight throughout the autumn months.

I was not sure how well other types of grapes would grow in our humid environment, especially in containers. My first planting was not successful. I planted them in large, 15 gallon containers and placed them against a southern facing wall. The plants hung on, but never seemed to thrive. Then they failed to break dormancy in autumn. On my second attempt, I moved my containers away from the wall and placed the containers in a small garden plot in my yard. With very little atten-

Pesticide Residue Ranking: #7 (imported grapes)

Nutritional Information

One cup of fresh grapes contains about 60 calories. Grapes are a good source of Vitamin A and Potassium.[1] Muscadine grapes are gaining in popularity for the high levels of Resveratrol found in their skin, pulp, and seeds. Resveratrol, found in red wine, is the compound believed to lower risk of coronary heart disease.[2]

---

1. USDA National Nutrient Database for Standard Reference, Release 20 (2007).
2. USDA Agriculture Research Service 2002. http://www.ars.usda.gov/is/pr/1997/971120.htm

tion, the vines have grown vigorously. I believe adequate air circulation made the difference between my first two attempts to grow grapes.

The greater challenge in growing grapes in containers, however, is in producing fruit. Pay special attention to container size for best production. Some bonsai gardeners have had great success in producing grapes, even on very small vines.

General Information

There are two main classifications of grape vines: True and Muscadine. European and American classifications are subcategories of true grapes. These are most easily distinguished by the way the fruit is arranged on the vine. True grapes grow in elongated clusters. Muscadine grapes grow in smaller clusters and are usually harvested one at a time. Muscadine grapes grow readily in the southeast. True grape vines are more vigorous in temperate climates. Grape plants are deciduous. Leaves of Muscadine grape plants are 3″–4″ across with three pointed, divided sections. Leaves of true grapes larger and heart shaped, about 4″–5″ wide. All grapes plants are vines. These can spread 25.′

Residue

Thirty four pesticide residues were found on imported grapes sampled by the USDA. A single sample of imported grapes tested positive for 14 pesticides. Pesticides detected most frequently included Cyprodinil, Imidacloprid and Captan.[18]

Variety Selection

Gardeners in the Southeast, extending from central and northern Florida along the Gulf of Mexico to Texas, and as far north as Missouri, should consider growing a muscadine variety. Pest and disease resistant, these vines are almost always grown without chemicals. Though Muscadine varieties have rather large seeds, they are prolific producers of sweet delicious fruit and grow readily in this region. Muscadine grapes also make delicious jellies.

European varieties grow well in temperate, dry climates. ***Flame*** is a popular variety for fresh eating.

Thompson is suitable for desert climates. In colder climates, consider ***Reliance*** or ***Canadice***.

Many grape varieties are self pollinating, or pollinate readily from plants

---

Botanical Name

Vitis vinifera
Family: *Viticeae*

Yield

Containerized grape vines typically bear 1–3 pounds of fruit per year.

---

[18]. USDA Pesticide Data Program, 2002.

several miles away. Pollination and temperature requirements are included in the chart below.

Note: Selecting grape cultivars involves more than temperature and pollination consideration. Some vines have day length and chill hour requirements. It is best to talk with local extension agents to determine the right grape variety for your growing area.

Other grape cultivars to consider: **Seneca** (yellow), **Delaware** (red), **Steuben** (blue-black), and **Niagara** (white).

Planting Dates

Bare root vines should be planted when dormant, in late winter or early spring.

Container Choice

Grapes have a tap root and need a very deep container. To have a chance at producing fruit, containers should be at least 15" deep.

Excellent drainage is especially important when growing grape vines. Add ¼" of gravel to the bottom of a container with at least three drainage holes.

Site Selection

As grapes are a vining plant, it is necessary to set up a trellis system for them prior to planting. Grape vines are usually trained to travel horizontally so keep this in mind when selecting a location for the plants. Because the plants will quickly grow onto any support they can reach, it is not easy to

Grape Varieties, Temperature & Pollinator Requirements		
"Muscadine" varieties	Minimum Temeratures Tolerated	Pollinator Required (Any self pollinating Muscadine cultivar will pollinate non-pollinating Muscadines)
Black Beauty	10°F	Carlos, Cowart, Nesbit
Scuppernog	10°F	Carlos, Cowart, Nesbit
Sweet Jenny	10°F	Carlos, Cowart, Nesbit
"True Grape" varieties	Minimum Temeratures Tolerated	Pollinator Required
Flame	10°F	NA
Thompson	10°F	NA
Reliance	−20°F	NA
Canadice	−20°F	NA
Concord	−20°F	NA

move the plants to other locations during inclement weather. It is important to select a site where the plants can grow year round. Supports with open sides provide greater air circulation than walls. The simplest, ready-built support is a chain link fence. Grape vines provide quick aesthetic improvement to these fences.

If a fence is not available, attach a trellis to a wall using supports spaced 4″–6″ from the wall to allow air circulation. If you are placing the containers outside on top of soil, posts, about 5′ tall, can be inserted into the ground on either side of a containerized grape plant. Wire can then be added for horizontal growth. Small trellises tied to the outside of a container or placed inside a container are adequate while the vine is young, but will need to be reinforced as the plant grows.

Planting Procedure

Select one-year bare root vines and plant about three weeks before the last frost. Trim the roots to 6.″ Prune the top of vine to 2–3 buds, cutting canes on an angle away from the center of the plant. Judging by the color change on the cane, you can usually determine how deeply the vine was planted at the nursery. Bury in the new container to the same depth. Grape vines are not usually affected negatively if they are planted a little deeper than their original container.

Soil

There are many differing opinions about the necessary quality and ingre-

> ### Optimum Growing Conditions
>
> - **Location/Sun Exposure:** Fruit production may be diminished in windy regions. Container gardeners should select a protected site for growing grape vines. Muscadine plants produce fruit in full sun to partial shade. True grapes should be planted in full sun to partial shade, depending on the temperature.
> - **Moisture:** Grape vines should be watered consistently, but the soil should be allowed to dry between waterings. To avoid excess moisture on the leaves and subsequent fungal conditions, consider drip irrigation.
> - **Temperature:** Muscadine grape vines: 10ºF and warmer. True grapes: See specific varieties in the chart above. Plants grown in a location protected from wind may thrive where the climate is otherwise too cold.

Fig. 7-1: Grape vine on chain link fence

dients of soil for grape plants, especially in the wine making industry. Average, but well-draining soil with a slightly acidic pH of 6.0–6.5 is generally considered ideal for grape production.

Fertilization

Grapes generally do not require a lot of fertilization. High levels of nitrogen will cause the plant to grow excessive foliage with little fruit production. A treatment with dilute organic fertilizer balanced to 10-10-10 in early spring is usually sufficient.

Pests & Diseases

Muscadine grapes have adapted over hundreds of years in the southeast and are fairly resistant to pests and diseases.

For prevention and treatment information, see chapter 14.

Pruning

Pruning is necessary to control growth and increase fruit production. After planting in early spring, allow the vine to grow until winter. In early winter, tie the strongest shoot to the support and prune it back to three buds. Remaining shoots should also be removed. Early the next spring, allow one of the shoots growing off the main leader to remain. (Remove all other shoots.) In the second summer, tip off the top of the main branch so the plant begins to grow horizontally. In mid-summer, select the two sturdiest shoots to tie to horizontal supports and prune off the others. The vine should look like a "T" formation. During the second winter, remove all growth from the main leaders and trunk. The vine will then be trained to a formation suitable for fruit production. In subsequent springs, thin any shoots growing off the main leader to 1' apart. Note: In later years, there will be additional pruning requirements of spurs or canes, specific to the cultivar you grow. These instructions should be included with the purchase of your plant.

Spur Pruning: In general, all Muscadine and a few other cultivars require spur pruning, or pruning of the side shoots. These should be pruned to about 8" apart and cut back to about two buds.

Cane Pruning: Cane pruning is recommended for Thompson, Concord, Flame and many other True grape cultivars. During the third winter, prune off all but twelve shoots closest to the

---

Some Grape Pests
- Grapeberry Moth
- Spider Mites
- Yellow Jacket Bees
- Birds

Some Grape Diseases
- Blackrot
- Mildew
- Anthracnose

trunk of the "T." These will be the shoots that produce fruiting canes in summer. Remove these canes the following winter as well as all but twelve shoots growing closest to the trunk.

© Barbara Barker

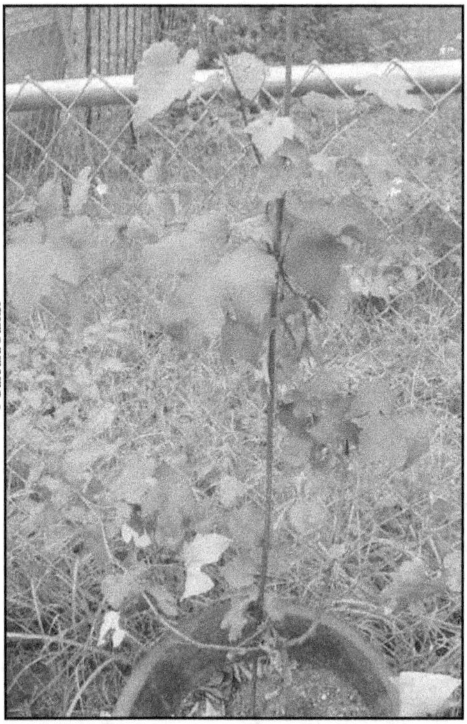

Fig. 7-2: Containerized grape vine

© Barbara Barker

Fig. 7-3: Muscadine grapes

With this method, fruit is produced on new shoots each year and old, less productive wood is removed.

Harvesting/Storage

There is an argument over whether harvesting grapes in vineyards is an art or a science. Old timers determine harvest by the color, taste, and softness of the grape. Other vineyards use technology to determine when sugar values are precisely correct for optimal harvest. In the case of home gardeners, I think we are all happy to pop a grape in our mouths and declare whether or not our grapes are ready for harvest. When the mature color has been reached and the grape has begun to soften, there is not much risk of getting dry mouth from an immature grape.

Refrigerated, grapes last about 5–10 days. Jellies, jams, and juice can be readily made from excess harvest.

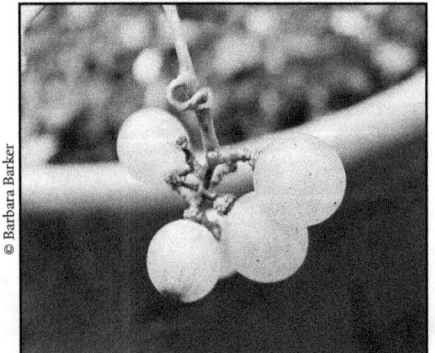

Chapter 8

SWEET BELL PEPPERS

One of the many surprises I experienced while living in Morocco occurred while visiting a villager in a mud hut with no electricity or running water. Sitting on the floor around a small gas stove, my friend Bouchra taught me how to skin a sweet bell pepper. She expertly blackened the skin over the flame and then scraped the softened skin with a sharp knife. I have seen the same method in numerous cooking magazines since. Good food doesn't have to come from expensive grocery stores and fancy kitchens!

Sweet bell peppers are not only delicious, but also beautiful in container gardens. An array of bright colors and sizes add pizzazz to the container garden. Luckily, they grow easily in con-

Pesticide Residue Ranking: #8

Nutritional Information

Though nutritional information differs according to the color, sweet bell peppers are a great source of Phosphorus, Potassium, Vitamin C, Niacin, Folate, Beta Carotene, and Lutein + zeaxanthin.

USDA National Nutrient Database for Standard Reference, Release 19 (2006).

Botanical Name

Capsicum annum

Family: *Solanaceae*

tainers and require very little maintenance. Sweet bell peppers might be considered the ideal container plant.

Peppers rank number eight on the Environmental Working Group's Dirty Dozen list, but the price of this brightly colored produce, about $3 a pound in my local grocery store, may be another reason to add these to your container garden. A 12-cent seed plus the cost of the soil, fertilizer, container and water will yield about four bell peppers. If all supplies must be purchased new, home grown peppers may not be cheaper than those from the grocery store. However, the use of recycled containers and homemade compost will bring the cost down to less than 50 cents per pepper.

Sweet bell peppers are perennial plants, but are grown as annuals in temperate climates. In containers, the growing season can be extended year round if plants are protected from frost and adequate warmth is provided. Plants have multiple branches and alternate leaves. Pepper plants grow 2′–4′ tall and wide. Bell pepper blossoms are small and white. They self pollinate, but can be cross-pollinated by bees and other insects. Fruit size depends on the variety, but averages 4″x4.″ They are usually propagated by seeds.

> **Recommended Container Varieties**
> - Jingle Bells, Apple (red)
> - Islander (lavender)
> - Mandarin (orange)
> - Ori (yellow)

> **Yield**
> Depends on variety. 5–6 plants per season are usually enough to supply a family of four. 8-10 weeks from transplanting to harvest.

> **Peppers & Tobacco**
> Due to the transmission of tobacco mosaic virus, pepper plants may be easily killed by contact with tobacco. Wash your hands before handling seed or soil if you have come into contact with any form of tobacco.

Residue

As with most blemish free, colorful produce, typical grocery store peppers have significant pesticide residues. Ranking number eight on the Environmental Working Group's "Dirty Dozen List," residues were found on 69% of all peppers tested by the USDA. Forty-nine different pesticides were found on the peppers tested. The three chemicals found most commonly on peppers (after washing and preparing) were Imidacloprid, Methamidophos and Carbendazim (MBC).

Seed Starting

Seeds are not too difficult to germinate, but the seedlings do require care for three to five weeks before they can be planted out into the garden. A wide variety of young plants are available at local garden centers and online if you wish to skip the seed stage.

Soil: Start seeds in one part each perlite, vermiculite, and potting soil. Dampen soil before planting.

Planting seeds: Place 1–2 seeds in each small pot or each cell of a flat. Cover seeds about ⅛" (3–4 mm) with horticultural vermiculite or soil mix. Spray gently with a spray bottle or mister. This will settle seeds and remove air pockets.

With a bottom heater, seeds will germinate faster and more consistently. These can be purchased from garden supply stores or catalogs. Otherwise cover the flats with plastic wrap and place in a warm, sunny window or under a fluorescent light hung a few inches above the pots or cells. Temperatures of 75°–80°F are ideal for germination. When the seedlings begin to emerge, remove the wrap and begin to bottom water by pouring a little water into the bottom of the flat.

Transplanting

After two sets of leaves have grown, the seedlings can be moved into larger containers, but should remain indoors until the weather is at least 75°F and there is no danger of frost. As with all seedlings, gradually introduce to outdoor conditions in increasingly longer periods of time.

Fig. 8-1: Newly planted cell packs. *with horticultural vermiculite covering seeds.*

Fig. 8-2: Recycled clamshell flat. *Originally held a pound of lettuce. As a "mini-greenhouse," holds 3 cell packs (6-packs).*

Fig. 8-3: Young pepper plants in a concrete container

Soil

Peppers grow well in average to rich garden soil. Some gardeners incorporate rock phosphate, greensand, or wood ashes to increase potash in the soil.

Growing On

Peppers prefer warm temperatures of 75°–85°F. Cool night temperatures cause blossoms to fall off. Any fruit grown from plants exposed to cold temperatures tends to be small and misshapen.

Peppers need consistent bottom watering. To prevent rust disease, I do not recommend top watering.

Fertilizing with dilute fish emulsion after blossoms have begun to appear will increase yields.

If temperatures rise above 85°F, move plants to a lightly shaded area. Apply a thick layer of grass clippings to prevent plants from losing too much moisture during hot, dry months. Keep the clippings about an inch from the stem of the plant.

Pests & Diseases

Due to the transmission of tobacco mosaic virus, pepper plants may be killed by contact with tobacco. Wash your hands before handling seed or soil if you have come into contact with any form of tobacco. Occasionally, peppers are affected by mosaic and anthracnose (rust) diseases.

Optimum Growing Conditions
- Full Sun (depending on variety)
- 1″ of water per week
- **Temperature:** Warm to hot. Apply mulch to maintain consistent root temperatures.

Some Pepper Pests & Diseases
- Cutworms
- Tobacco Mosaic Virus
- anthracnose (rust)

Fig. 8-4: Containerized pepper plant

Other than cutworms, you will have very few insect pest problems with peppers. When placing pepper plants into their permanent containers, surround each stem with a stiff paper collar. This will prevent cutworms from munching on your plants.

See chapter 14 for more information on preventing and treating for pests and diseases.

Harvesting

Peppers increase their vitamin C content in the final stages of development, so it is best to leave them on the plant until their mature color is reached. Peppers are ready to harvest when they are firm to touch and feel heavy. Cut peppers from the plant (don't twist or pick them), about ½" up the stem from the top of the pepper. Peppers can be stored for up to about 30 days when picked green and kept humid at about 32°F.

Chapter 9

POTATOES

Growing potatoes in containers is a great way to reduce pest related risks to your crop. It also permits a longer growing season.

Growing your own potatoes opens up a world of colors, sizes, and flavors not available in most grocery stores.

General Information

Potatoes are tubers grown from perennial plants. Potato plants are low-growing, with white flowers and yellow stamens. Plants are propagated by planting divisions of the potato and its "eyes." Potatoes are informally classified into two main groups: "new" or "fingerlings" and the larger "main" or "earlies."

Solanine Toxicity

There is much folklore about the ill

Pesticide Residue Ranking: #9

Nutritional Information

One medium potato (213 grams) contains 153 calories and is an excellent source of magnesium, iron, potassium, fiber, vitamin C, & niacin.

USDA National Nutrient Database for Standard Reference, Release 20 (2007).

Yield

Yield varies by variety, container size, and whether the plants received consistent water. Five pounds per trash-can sized container is generally considered a good yield.

effects of eating green potatoes. I've researched this as much as possible and found a small amount of truth about the toxicity of potatoes.

> ### Botanical Name
> *Solanum tuberosum*
>
> Family: *Solanaceae*

> ### Some Potato Varieties
>
> **Early** (About 60 days to harvest)
> - **Red Norland** (Very Early; Red)
> - **Bintje** (Yellow; heirloom)
> - **Caribe** (Purple)
>
> **Mid** (About 75 days to harvest)
> - **Desiree** (European gourmet; red; oblong)
> - **Fabula** (Yellow; low-carb)
> - **Rote Erstling** (my favorite, but better for northern climates; Red skin, yellow flesh)
> - **Yellow Finn** (European gourmet; yellow; flat and round)
>
> **Late** (Up to 100 days to harvest)
> - **Golden Sunburst** (Yellow skin and flesh)
> - **Romance** (Light red skin, yellow flesh)
>
> **Fingerlings**
> - **French fingerling** (Early; European gourmet; red skin, yellow flesh)
> - **Larotte** (Mid to late; Very smooth & creamy; preferred by chefs; tan skin, yellow flesh)

Potatoes are known to contain a toxic glycoalkaloid called solanine. There has not been a documented case of solanine poisoning from potatoes in the U.S. in fifty years. Selective cultivar breeding has reduced solanine concentrations.

In high concentrations, solanine primarily causes headaches, nausea, fatigue, diarrhea and vomiting. In extremely high concentrations it can cause much more severe symptoms. Wild potatoes contain higher concentrations of these substances than cultivated potatoes. Solanine concentrations are higher in potatoes exposed to light (chlorophyll) while growing and in spoiled potatoes (after harvest).[19] Cooking potatoes at temperatures over 340°F is said to destroy most of these toxic compounds. Green potatoes often have higher concentrations of these compounds. There is not much to worry about here, though. One would have to consume 4–9 fresh potatoes at a time to experience a dangerous dose of these compounds.[20]

Residue

Potatoes rank number nine on the Environmental Working Group's list of the Dirty Dozen. Thirty seven pes-

---

19. cf Andrew Montario, "Potato Glycoalkaloid Toxicity Solanine," (April 1999).

20. cf Marita Cantwell, "A Review of Important Facts about Potato Glycoalkaloids," UC Davis. http://ucce.ucdavis.edu/files/datastore/234-182.pdf

ticides were detected on fresh potato samples after they had been cleaned and prepared for eating. Residue of Methamidophos and Phorate Sulfone were found most commonly.

Variety Selection

In addition to traditional waxy (boiling) and fluffy (baking) potatoes, there is the French fingerling, purple, cranberry, gold, white, and a few hundred others! Peruse the various seed potato websites or catalogs and choose varieties that suit your cooking needs.

Always purchase certified seed potatoes. Certification ensures potatoes are free of disease and pests. Uncertified potatoes are usually meant for eating and are likely to have been sprayed with a growth inhibitor.

Planting Dates

Potatoes need long periods of cool weather. Cold-climate gardeners may plant early maturing potatoes no earlier than 6–8 weeks before the last expected frost. After that date, plant as soon as the ground has begun to thaw but is no longer soggy. Container gardeners do not need to worry about wet, frozen soil and can get a jump on the season. A second crop of mid to late potatoes can be planted in late spring for a fall crop.

Warm climate gardeners often plant as early as January for a spring crop and again in September for a fall crop. In USDA plant hardiness zones 8–10, plant earlies in fall and over-winter for a very early harvest in spring. Later varieties can be planted from mid-March to April.

The main consideration is planting potato plants early enough to avoid hot, wet periods during the potatoes' maturation phase.

Container Choice

Containers should be at least 18″ wide by 30″ tall. Though I've seen potatoes grown in smaller containers, twenty gallon garbage cans are consid-

---

Optimum Growing Conditions

- **Location/Sun Exposure:** Potato plants require full sun. Provide shelter from high winds.

- **Moisture:** Consistent moisture is important when growing potatoes. Drought conditions followed by heavy rains cause potatoes to crack so it is best to place potato pots in an area where you can control moisture levels. To determine if soil is watered deeply enough, dig down 8″–10″ and feel the soil. If it is moist, your plants are watered adequately. If it is wet or dry, adjust your watering schedule accordingly.)

- **Temperature:** Soil temperature must be at least 45ºF for plants to develop. Maximum production occurs when soil temperatures range from 60º–70ºF during the growing season. Potatoes will not form when soil temperatures rise above 80ºF.

ered ideal for growing potatoes.

I have never understood the fascination with growing potatoes in tires. However, it is a popular choice so I provide detailed instructions below.

- **Wooden Cage:** Irish Eyes Garden Seeds offers a detailed plan for constructing a wooden cage for growing potatoes (visit **www.gardencityseeds.net/growers1.php**).
- **Garbage Can:** Drill 3–5 holes in the bottom of the can for drainage. Follow planting instructions in the 'planting procedure' section of this chapter.
- **Tires:** Place a tire on the ground or on a gravel path. Fill it with soil and plant the potatoes within the tire. When the potato plants are 3″–4″ tall, add a second tire on top of the first, add soil around the plant, up to the top 2″ of the leaves. Add soil to this level on the plant as the plants grow. Additional tires can be added as the plants grow, but always leave 2″ of leaves above the surface of the soil. See the 'planting procedure' section of this chapter for more on cultivating potatoes.

Soil

Potato plants tolerate a variety of soils. They are most vigorous in a well-draining loam. Begin with vegetable garden soil and incorporate a bag of humus. Mix in fertilizer (see fertilization section in the next page). Preferred pH: 5.2–6.8.

Planting Procedure

- **Chitting:** A week before planting, lay potatoes, eye clusters up, out on a newspaper in filtered light (bright shade) and allow them to sprout. This will speed up the germination process. When eyes have 1″ long green sprouts, the potatoes are ready to plant.
- **Preparing potatoes:** Small potatoes can be planted whole. Larg-

Fig. 9-1: Potato shoots

er potatoes should be cut into 2" pieces. Each piece should have at least three eyes. To ward off scab and other diseases, some organic gardeners dust their potato pieces with sulphur before planting.

- **Planting:** Fill 1/3 of container with soil. Spacing potatoes 6" apart, lay them on the surface of the soil, 4" away from the sides of the container. Cover with 2" of soil. When plants are 6" high, add soil up to the top 2" of the plant. Allow the plant to grow another 6" and then bury it up to the top 2" again. Continue this practice until soil is 2" from top of container. It is important to keep potatoes buried. Exposure to sun will cause them to green.
- **Watering:** Water thoroughly at planting time and continue to keep soil moist, but not soggy, throughout growing season.

Fertilization

Select a low nitrogen fertilizer, such as cottonseed meal and combine this with compost. Apply in small amounts (1 part compost/cottonseed: 100 parts soil). Over-fertilizing will result in decreased potato production and increased production of leaves.

Pests and Diseases

When it comes to preventing disease and discouraging pests, container

Some Potato Pests
- Colorado Potato Beetle
- Aphids
- Leafhoppers
- Flea Beetles
- Wireworms

Some Potato Diseases
- Blight
- Scab

gardeners have a big advantage over traditional gardeners. However, it is always wise to be on the lookout for critters and moisture related diseases. For prevention and treatment information, see Chapter 14.

Harvesting & Storage

If you prefer small "new" potatoes, harvest when plants flower, about 8 weeks after planting. (Some plants don't flower so you will need to keep track of planting dates.) For mature potatoes, harvest when flowers die. Using a garden fork, dig down into the soil about 10" from the potato plant. Gently lift the entire plant. Pull potatoes from the vines. Place potatoes in burlap bags, away from sunlight. These bags can often be purchased at local feed stores. Keep in a cool environment (50°–60°F) for two weeks. Then examine the potatoes and store only bruise and blemish-free potatoes. Stored in a well ventilated area at 40°F, potatoes will keep 3–6 months.

Chapter 10

BLUEBERRIES

A perennial, the blueberry is a tall shrub, ranging in size from 8" to 5' tall. Depending on the cultivar and climate, the leaves can be deciduous or evergreen and range from 1/3" long to 3" long. Two main species, Highbush and Lowbush are propagated by home gardeners. Mature fruit is a reddish to purple berry, 1/4"–1/2" in diameter.

Varieties

Four main varieties of blueberry are grown in North America: Northern Highbush (V. corymbosum), Southern Highbush (interspecific hybrids of V. darrowi, V. ashei and V. corymbosum), Southern Rabbiteye (V. ashei), and Lowbush (V. angustifolium). Northern Highbush is the most commonly grown

Pesticide Residue Ranking: #10 (domestic blueberries)

Nutritional Information

Nutritional Data: One cup of blueberries contains 84 calories. Blueberries are an excellent source of Dietary Fiber, Vitamin C, Vitamin K, Manganese and antioxidants.

for in-depth nutritional information, search "blueberries" at Nutrition Data, http://nutritiondata.self.com

Botanical Name

Vaccinium angustifolium

cultivar in North America. Its range is from Nova Scotia to Alabama. Southern Highbush, a cultivar of Northern Highbush, is productive in warm climates, primarily in the southeastern United States. Rabbiteye is grown in cooler regions of the southeast, ranging from the Carolinas to northern regions of Florida and Texas. Lowbush is a wild blueberry found in the Northeastern United States. Due to their large size and nutrient requirements, these varieties are generally not recommended for container gardens. A few cultivars, however, have recently been bred for containers. Sunshine Blue is a warm climate container choice. Northsky grows best in cold climates. Bluecrop and Earliblue are recommended for arid climates. Tophat is a dwarf variety. It grows well in mild climates, ranging from North Florida to Virginia. Grow two varieties for best fruit production.

Residue

Blueberries rank number 10 on the Environmental Working Group's Dirty Dozen list. Fifty two different pesticides were found on blueberries after they were washed and prepared for eating. Boscalid, Pyraclostrobin, Cyprodinil and Iprodione were found most commonly.[21]

---

21. USDA Pesticide Data Program, http://www.ams.usda.gov/AMSv1.0/pdp

Climate

There is a variety for nearly all climates. See specific information in the section on varieties.

Container Choice

Plant blueberry in a pot at least 1/3 larger than the rootball. Blueberry is shallow-rooted so depth is not as important as diameter. Blueberry likes moist soil, but quickly dies in overly wet containers. Drill three holes in the bottom of the pot if it does not already have drainage holes. In the field, Blueberry is often planted on the top layer of soil-free, pine bark mulch raised beds. Filling a container with pinebark mulch and barely covering the roots may be a successful method of growing blueberry plants.

Soil

Unlike most plants, Blueberry will only grow in acidic soil. Deficiencies in zinc, iron and mircro-elements occur in higher pH soils. Mix a small amount of granulated sulfur in your potting soil to create acidic conditions before planting. Mulch with pine needles or pine bark to maintain soil acidity.

Fertilization

Over-fertilization will kill blueberry plants. Blueberry is not a big nitrogen feeder and absorbs nitrogen in the ammonium form best. Fishmeal remains ammoniated longer than other fertilizers and is a good choice for organic gardeners. Other fertilizers may lower pH and inhibit nutrient uptake by blueberry plants.

Moisture

Most blueberry cultivars die quickly in dry conditions. Set drip irrigation to water blueberry plants in the morning so the plant has a chance to dry before nightfall. Cold, wet roots will stress blueberry plants. Roots should be thoroughly moistened every day, but soil should be well-draining and should allow the roots to dry slightly before the next watering.

Harvesting

Blueberries are harvested when the fruit is plump and no longer reddish in color. Harvest times are determined by dates of the last frost, but fruit usually ripens when temperatures exceed 800°F.

Pests & Diseases[22]

Reduce blueberry pests and diseases by growing varieties recommended for your area, providing ample circulation around your plants and by keeping the leaves as dry as possible. Placing pots in a sheltered location and utilizing drip irrigation will eliminate fungal diseases on your plants. As with most pests and diseases, growing blueberry plants in containers provides protection from most of the problems commercial growers have to spray to control.

Some Blueberry Diseases:

- Phytophtora root rot
- Botrytis flower blight (gray mold)
- Blueberry stem blight

Some Blueberry Pests:

- Flea beetles
- Scale
- Cranberry fruitworms
- Caterpillars
- Root weevils
- Blueberry gall midge
- Birds, including Cedar wax wings, robins and crows

---

22. University of Florida IFAS Extension, http://edis.ifas.ufl.edu/mg359

Chapter 11

Lettuce is one of my favorite foods to grow in containers. I experience such a feeling of satisfaction when I walk past high priced, bagged lettuce in the store. With literally hundreds of varieties to grow, some more heat tolerant than others, you can grow lettuce in all but the hottest months outside and throughout the year inside your home. When you grow your own lettuce, you will discover more textures, colors, and flavors of lettuce then you ever imagined. Very little effort is required to grow lettuce. Just toss a few seeds in a pot and soon you will be feeling smug when you walk past the lettuce section of your supermarket too.

General Information

Lettuce adds a lot of color to con-

Pesticide Residue Ranking: #11

Nutritional Information

Six leaves of Romaine lettuce contains twenty calories. Lettuce is an excellent source of Vitamin A and Fiber.

USDA National Nutrient Database for Standard Reference, Release 20 (2007).

Yield

Yield varies greatly by lettuce type. One 12" pot of loose leaf lettuce will provide a family of four with a nice sized salad every 3–4 weeks.

tainer gardens. I like to sow a mixture of varieties in large pots for the ornamental value. Careful variety selection and successive sowing enables container gardeners to keep a ready supply of lettuce throughout most of the year.

Like most greens, lettuce is a cool season annual. There are four main groups of lettuce: Crisphead, Butterhead, Leaf lettuce, and Romaine.

- **Crisphead lettuce** grows leaves in a tight round ball with crisp leaves, such as iceberg lettuce
- **Butterhead lettuce**, or Bibb lettuce, is also a head lettuce, but the leaves are softer and they form a looser bunch than Crisphead lettuces. The photo at the top of this chapter is a butterhead.
- **Leaf lettuce** does not form a head. The leaves are curly and grow in a long bunch.
- **Romaine lettuce** varieties (also known as Cos) also do not form a head. Romaine leaves grow upright and are thicker, coarser, and darker green than most other lettuces.

Any type of lettuce can be grown in containers. Leaf lettuce may be the most container friendly choice.

Residue

After samples were washed and prepared for eating, 51 pesticide residues were found on lettuce samples tested by the USDA. Imidacloprid, DCPA and Dimethomorph were found most frequently on samples.

Botanical Name
Lactuca sativa

Favorite Crisphead Varieties
Nevada & Sierra
Crisphead varieties are the toughest to grow due to their long growing season. Nevada and Sierra are heat tolerant and more flavorful than Iceberg.

Favorite Butterhead Varieties
- Buttercrunch is heat tolerant.
- Tom Thumb grows well in containers due to its compact nature.

Favorite Leaf Lettuce Varieties
- Blackseeded Simpson has excellent flavor and large green leaves.
- Lolla Rosa has red tips and curly leaves.
- Red Sails, Salad Bowl, and Lolla Rosa are more heat tolerant than other leaf varieties.

Favorite Romaine Variety
Little Gem
A dwarf variety, good for containers.

Planting Dates

Lettuce grows best in a temperature range of 45°–65°F. If you are gardening indoors, lettuce can be grown year round. Sow new seeds every two weeks for a constant supply. This is known as "succession cropping."

For outdoor container gardening, aim for those times of year when temperatures range from a little below freezing to about 75°F. In most regions, this means outdoor direct seeding should be done in early spring or early fall. Extend the harvest season further into the summer by succession sowing every two weeks, placing containers in partial shade, and by planting heat tolerant lettuce varieties and other greens, such as Malabar spinach.

Another way to extend the outdoor harvest season is to sow seeds indoors, and later move seedlings outdoors. This gives them a head-start. For a spring crop using this method, start seedlings indoors 5–6 weeks before the last frost date. Transplant to the outdoors or move containers outdoors after danger of freezing temperatures is past. Light frost will not harm lettuce. For an outdoor fall crop, sow seeds indoors 5–6 weeks before temperatures are expected to generally remain below 75°F outside. Move plants outdoors when the cooler weather arrives.

Container Choice

Lettuce is shallow rooted, so containers 10″ deep are sufficient. If growing large headed lettuces, containers should be 12″–15″ wide.

Though lettuce needs a moist soil, good drainage is important. Use containers with at least three drainage holes.

> **Other Favorite Greens**
>
> Arugula, endive, escarole, spinach, and chicory are not technically lettuces, but make excellent salad additions and can be grown in containers.

Planting Procedure

Lettuce seeds are heat sensitive and will not germinate if exposed to extreme heat. Store them in a cool, dark location. Place seeds in refrigera-

Fig. 11-1: Lettuce in raised growing bed

tor overnight prior to sowing. This will break the seeds' dormancy.

Lettuce seeds need some light to germinate. It is best to leave them uncovered when planting. Scatter seeds in container and lightly press them into the soil.

Lettuce consists primarily of water, so it is crucial to keep soil uniformly moist from sowing to harvest. As plants grow, thin to 2" apart and later to 4"–6" apart. Add the thinnings to your salads.

Soil

Lettuce grows best in fertile soil. To a commercial bag of vegetable potting soil, add a bag of composted cow manure. Mix in well, making sure to break up all large pieces.

Fertilization

Lettuce tastes better when grown quickly. It is a fairly heavy feeder so begin with a rich soil and top dress with a nitrogen-rich fertilizer or apply fish emulsion (diluted 50%) when plants reach 2" tall. If successive gardening (planting one crop after another), top dress with compost every 4–6 weeks.

Harvesting & Storage

I prefer to grow leaf and romaine lettuce varieties because their leaves can be picked from the main bunch throughout the growing season. Crispheads and butterheads are picked at full maturity in one large bunch. To harvest full plant, cut all leaves 1" above soil surface. The plants will grow again.

Optimum Growing Conditions

- **Location/Sun Exposure:** In cold climates, place containers in full sun. In all other areas, lettuce grows best in partial sun.
- **Moisture:** Lettuce prefers a consistently moist, but not soggy soil. This is critical for production. In windy climates, extra watering will be necessary.
- **Temperature:** Lettuces typically do not germinate in temperatures above 75°F. Most lettuces will become bitter in temperatures above 80°F. Lettuce will continue to grow even through light frosts.

Pests & Diseases

Pests: Lettuce is most commonly affected by slugs, snails, and aphids.

Diseases: Lettuce is mildly susceptible to downy mildew and fusarium wilt.

For prevention and treatment information, see chapter 14.

Chapter 12

There are few foods lower in calories and higher in nutritional value than Kale. It grows easily in containers and provides a splash of color and texture to cool weather gardens.

Description

Kale, commonly called "greens," varies from cream to purple to red. It is closely related to Collards and Brussels Sprouts. Depending on the variety, leaves range in size from 12″–24″ long and 8″–15″ wide. In some varieties, leaf edges curl. Usually grown as an annual, Kale is actually a biennial.

Residue

Kale ranked 12 on the Environmental Working Group's list of the dirty dozen. Up to 16 different pesticide

Pesticide Residue Ranking: #12

Nutritional Information

At just 33 calories per cup, Kale is an excellent source of Vitamins A, C, & K.

Search "kale" at http://nutritiondata.self.com
Also search the USDA National Nutritient Database, www.nal.usda.gov/fnic/foodcomp/search/

Botanical Name

Brassica oleracea
var. *acephala*

residues were found on approximately 41% of samples in a 2007 USDA study. Pesticides most commonly found were DDE p,p1 and DDT p,p1.

Prior to testing, produce was washed and prepared for eating.

Climate

Kale prefers cool temperatures. The flavor of kale even benefits from a touch of frost. Optimal soil temperature is 60°–65°F. Hot weather turns kale bitter.

Seed Starting

Start seeds indoors six weeks before last frost or wait until spring and direct seed in outdoor containers. Warm climate gardeners can grow Kale in the fall. Winter crops produce sweeter leaves. Kale seeds germinate in approximately one week. Cover seeds with about ½" of soil and don't allow the seeds to dry out before germinating. Kale is sometimes prone to moisture related diseases so bottom watering is recommended. Soil should be kept moist, but not soggy.

Transplant seedlings after danger of frost has passed. Space plants approximately 16" apart.

For a continuous supply, sow seeds every three weeks during the growing season.

Container Choice

Plant Kale in 6"–10" deep by 36" wide containers. Though kale needs a moist soil, good drainage is still important. Use containers with at least three holes.

Soil

Kale prefers a rich soil, high in organic matter. pH should be slightly acidic (5.5–6.5). Mulch with pine straw or pine bark to increase acidity.

Fertilization

Kale is a heavy feeder. High nitrogen levels will increase growth rate and size of leaves, but may also attract aphids. To a commercial bag of organic vegetable potting soil, add a bag of composted cow manure. Mix in well, making sure to break up all large pieces. Top dress kale with compost throughout the growing season. Top dress with compost weekly after plants are well established.

Harvesting & Storage

From seed, Kale is ready for harvest in 70–80 days. Outside leaves can be harvested once 8"–10" high. To harvest the entire plant, cut 2" above the soil and the plant will sprout new leaves in approximately two weeks. Young kale is more tender and sweet than older leaves.

Optimum Growing Conditions

- **Location/Sun Exposure:** In warm climates, plant kale in partial shade. In cooler climates, plant in full sun.

- **Moisture:** Kale prefers a consistently moist, but not soggy soil. This is critical for leaf production. In windy climates, extra watering may be necessary.
- **Temperature:** Germinate at 70°–75°F. Optimal growing temperatures is 60°–65°F. However, Kale can tolerate colder temperatures for short periods. Kale develops a bitter taste in warmer temperatures.

Pests & Diseases

Understanding the life cycle of pests is key to organic gardening. This knowledge allows the home gardener to prevent infestations by interrupting the development and movement of pests before they can destroy crops. Below are a few of the pests and diseases most commonly affecting Kale. A guide for prevention and organic treatments for pests and diseases is included in chapter 14.

Cabbage Worms & Loopers

Prevalent in all of North America, Cabbage Worms have additional generations in southern climates, where they are able to overwinter. Hemispherical eggs are yellow white to green in color and are laid singly or in clusters on the tops and bottoms of leaves.

Young larvae are white and hairy caterpillars. They turn darker green and lose their hair as they mature. Cocoons are formed on the undersides of foilage, in plant debris and in the soil. Small gray-brown moths emerge and lay approximately 500 eggs in their short adulthood of 10–15 days.

Prevention: Floating row covers effectively prevent cabbage loopers from laying eggs on the leaves of Kale.

Treatment: Bacillus thuringiensis and the release of parasitic wasps are moderately effective treatments.

Root Maggots

Root maggots are found throughout North America. Eggs are small and white and are usually laid in spring in plant stems at the soil line. Once hatched, larvae burrow down into the soil, feeding on plant seeds and young roots. Root maggots cause plant stunting and often death of early season vegetable plants.

Maggots are about 1/4" long with tapered heads. Adults emerge as dark gray flies that look like the common housefly, only smaller.

The tunneling action of maggots presents an additional risk to plants via diseases such as root and black rot.

Though most potent in early spring, several generations of root maggot can grow in one year.

Prevention: In areas with high humidity time plantings so harvests do not occur in times of highest humidity (for example, August in Florida.) Where possible, delay seed sowing until mid-spring. Allow plenty of air circulation between plants. Cover plants with row covers after sowing seeds. Place paper collars around young plants to protect the stems. Change the soil in containers each season. Maintaining a pH of 6.8 or higher discourages club root.

Treatment: Beneficial Nematodes.

Aphids

Aphids (*Hemiptera: Aphididae*) are tiny, pear-shaped, soft-bodied insects. There are approximately 4,400 aphid species in the world. The life cycle of aphids is amazing, but also vexing. Aphids are capable of reproducing via egg laying as wellas live birth. They engage in sexual and non-sexual reproduction.

Aphids have a piercing and sucking mouthpart. They suck sap from the leaves of plants, causing leaf curl and distortion. Sap excreted onto the leaves becomes a host for sooty mold. Aphids are also virus vectors. Viruses are transmitted to plants via their piercing mouthpiece.

Prevention: Row covers, slow release organic fertilizers, and mulching are effective measures for preventing aphids. The contrast in color between plant and soil provides a visual attraction to aphids. Applying row covers and mulching reduces the color differences. Aphids are especially attracted to sudden flushes of new growth. Steady release of nutrients via compost and organic fertilizers provides a slow and steady rate of growth.

Treatment: Aphids are easily removed in a home container garden by a strong spray of water from the hose. Insecticidal soap and horticultural oils are also effective.

Botrytis (Head Rot)

This is a fungus most commonly found in climates with high humidity. Botrytis begins as a gray mold on the foliage and eventually turns the leaves black.

Prevention: Avoid wetting the leaves. Water at the ground level or bottom water.

Treatment: First, remove and discard infected leaves. To prevent spread to the rest of the plant, try this baking soda treatment:

To one quart of water, add a drop of dish soap and a teaspoon of baking soda. Spray the tops and undersides of all leaves.

Chapter 13

PRIMARY PESTICIDES FOUND ON THE DIRTY DOZEN

Pesticides found on the Dirty Dozen are listed in this chapter along with their intended action.[23] There is debate about the level of health hazard created by these pesticides in humans. While I do not claim to be an expert on how these chemicals affect human health, I do think it makes sense to eliminate as many chemicals from my family's diet as possible.

Exposure data is gathered by the EPA in large part to protect farm workers. Information regarding acute toxicity included in the chart below refers to symptoms associated with direct contact in large amounts with the chemical. Chronic toxicity refers to exposure in lesser amounts over an extended period of time.

---

23. Sources for entire chapter:
"Extension Toxicology Network Pesticide Information Profiles," Oregon State University (June 1996), http://extoxnet.orst.edu/pips/ghindex.html

"Breast Cancer and Environmental Risk Factors," Prepared by Suzanne Snedeker, Ph.D. BCERF Associate Director for Translational Research, Cornell University (June 26, 2002), http://envirocancer.cornell.edu/FactSheet/General/fs45.chemical.cfm

U.S. EPA Pesticide Fact Sheets. National Pesticide Information Center, "Pesticide Fact Sheets," http://npic.orst.edu

PAN Pesticides Database, "Chemicals," http://www.pesticideinfo.org

Pesticide Data Table

Chemical	Description	Action
Acephate Trade Names: Orthene,™ Lancer,™ Pinpoint,™ Payload™	Organophosphate Foliar Spray	Controls Aphids, leafminers, caterpillars, sawflies, and thrips by disrupting the central nervous system. Symptoms of toxicity include headache, nervousness, blurred vision, weakness, nausea, cramps, diarrhea, difficulty breathing, and chest pain. The signs associated with acephate poisoning include sweating, pin-point pupils, tearing, salivation, clear nasal discharge and sputum, vomiting, muscle twitching, muscle weakness, and in severe poisonings convulsions, coma, and death.
Azinthos methyl Trade Names: Azimil,™ Bay 9027, Bay 17147, Carfene, Cotnion-methyl,™ Gusathion, Gusathion-M, Guthion,™ & Methyl-Guthion.	Organophosphate Foliar Spray	Controls leaf feeding insects. Works as a contact insecticide and a contact poison. Highly toxic by inhalation, dermal absorption, ingestion, and eye contact. Studies indicate chronic exposure causes impaired concentration and memory, and cause headache, irritability, nausea, vomiting, muscle cramps, and dizziness.
Bupirimate Trade Names: Brolly, Denarin, Funginex,™ Nimrod T, Saprol, & Triforine DC	Piperazine derivative used as a systemic fungicide	Control of powdery mildew, rusts, black rot and scab on cereals, fruit, ornamentals, and vegetables. Triforine is also active against storage diseases of fruit and suppresses red spider mite activity. Because of its low hazard to beneficial insects, triforine may be used in Integrated Pest Management (IPM) programs.
Captan Trade Names: Orthocide,™ Captan,™ Captan 400, Merpan,™ Vondcaptan	Chloroalkylthio fungicide	Controls fungal diseases on a wide variety of crops. The U.S. EPA has assigned captan a carcinogenicity classification of B2, a probable human carcinogen.
Chlorpyrifos Trade Names: Brodan, Detmol UA, Dowco 179, Dursban,™ Empire, Eradex, Lorsban,™ Paqeant, Piridane, Scout, & Stipend™	Broad spectrum Organophosphate insecticide	Controls cutworms, corn rootworms, cockroaches, grubs, flea beetles. Acute exposure: Chlorpyrifos is moderately toxic to humans. Poisoning from chlorpyrifos may affect the central nervous system, the cardiovascular system, and the respiratory system. It is also a skin and eye irritant. Chronic exposure: Symptoms similar to those of acute exposure.
Cyprodinil Technical, Vangard WP Fungicide	Fungicide	Controls Scab and Brown Rot Blossom. EPA classifies this chemical as "Not acutely toxic."

Chemical	Description	Action
DDE p.p	Break-down product of DDT by environmental degradation or metabolism.[24]	DDT has been illegal in the U.S. for decades. However, DDE still exists in the soil due to the widespread use of DDT before it was removed from the market. DDT is believed to still be in use in other countries. Positive residue on imported vegetables has occurred in recent years. Presence of DDE in women's and other mammals' breast milk is widespread.[25]
Diazenon Trade names: Basudin, Dazze,™ Gardentox, Kayazol, Knox Out, Nucidol, and Spectracide™	Organophosphate	Used to control leaf eating and sucking insects and yellow-jackets. Works by interfering with central nervous system. Classified as a restricted pesticide due to its devastating effects on bird populations. Acute toxicity includes weakness, headaches, tightness in the chest, blurred vision, nonreactive pinpoint pupils, salivation, sweating, nausea, vomiting, diarrhea, abdominal cramps, and slurred speech. Chronic effects include enzyme inhibition in red blood cells, in blood plasma, and in brain cells.
Diphenylamine NIPA,™ Anilinobenzene; Big Dipper; Biphenylamine; DFA; DPA; C.I. 10355; difenylamin; N,N-diphenylamine; N-fenylanilin; No Scald	Plant growth regulator	Used to control storage scald post harvest. Considered toxic to fish and aquatic invertebrates; Not considered to be highly toxic to humans.
Endosulfans Trade Name: Thiodan™	Contact insecticide and acaracide	Primarily affects the nervous system of mite pests. Exposure of endolsulfans "exceeds the agency's (EPA's) concerns for ...population subgroup, children ages 1–6."[26]
Fenhexamid Trade Names: Captevate,™ Elevate	Fungicide; Analide	Used primarily on fruit crops.
Iprodione	Contact fungicide	Used on a wide variety of plants including fruit and root crops. Considered a "slightly toxic" compound.

---

24. Environmental Protection Agency, "healtheffects ccl2-reg2 dde," http://www.scribd.com/doc/2042417/Environmental-Protection-Agency-healtheffects-ccl2reg2-dde

25. "DDT/DDE," Breast Cancer Fund, http://www.breastcancerfund.org

26. Environmental Protection Agency, http://www.epa.gov/pesticides/reregistration/REDs/factsheets/endosulfan_fs.htm.

Chemical	Description	Action
Malathion	Organophosphate	Works by interfering with the nervous system of pests. Malathion is not considered toxic. However, it metabolizes to malaoxon in humans. Acute exposure: High levels—symptoms include skin and eye irritation, cramps, nausea, diarrhea, excessive sweating, seizures and even death. Most symptoms tend to resolve within several weeks. Malathion present in untreated water is converted to malaoxon during the chlorination phase of water treatment, so malathion should not be used in waters that may be used as a source for drinking water, or any upstream waters. Chronic exposure: Some believe Maloxon impairs memory, but this is disputed. There is currently no reliable information on adverse health effects of chronic exposure to malathion.[27]
Methamidophos Trade Name: Monitor	Broad Spectrum Organophosphate	Used as an insecticide on tomatoes and potatoes in the U.S. and on peppers, strawberries, and squash in other countries. "Causes neurotoxic effects at low concentrations following both acute and chronic exposure. Organophosphates affect the nervous system by inhibiting acetylcholinesterase, an enzyme essential for normal nerve impulse transmission. Acetylcholinesterase inhibition causes acute effects in humans and other mammals. The symptoms in humans may include headache, exhaustion and mental confusion together with blurred vision, sweating, salivation, chest tightness, muscle twitching, and abdominal cramps. The more severe effects can include muscle paralysis leading to severe difficulty in breathing, so requiring respiratory support. Convulsions and unconsciousness can occur."[28]
Methomyl Brand Names: Cinate, Agrinate, DuPont 1179, Flytek, Kipsin, Lannate, Lanox, Memilene, Methavin, Methomex, Nudrin, NuBait, Pillarmate, & SD 14999	Carbamate	Used as foliar treatment on fruit, vegetable, and field crops. Classified by EPA as highly toxic. Symptoms of acute toxicity include weakness, blurred vision, stomach, and respiratory distress. Symptoms of chronic toxicity include inhibition of cholineserase and flu-like symptoms.

27. cf. Wikipedia, http://en.wikipedia.org/wiki/Malathion
28. Environmental Protection Authority, New Zealand. "Methamidophos Evaluation Sheet, Candidate for Re-Assessment Priority Listing."

Chemical	Description	Action

Mevinphos
 	
Trade Names: Apavinphos,™ CMDP, ENT 22374, Fosdrin, Gesfid, Meniphos,™ Menite, Mevinox, Mevinphos, OS-2046, PD5, Phosdrin & Phosfene
	Organophosphate	Used to control aphids, grasshoppers, leafhoppers, cutworms, caterpillars and other insects on fruit and vegetable crops. Classified by EPA has highly toxic. Also an acaracide for control of mites and ticks.
		    Symptoms of acute toxicity include neurological, respiratory and cardiac disorder.
		    Symptoms of chronic toxicity are similar to those of acute toxicity.

Parathion methyl	Organophosphate Compound	Banned in twenty three countries, Parathion methyl is considered extremely toxic. Indoor use is banned in the U.S. EPA is phasing out use of this chemical on most crops. Symptoms of acute toxicity include convulsions, unconsciousness, cardiac arrest, and death. Symptoms of chronic toxicity include persistent lack of appetite, weakness, and malaise.
Phorate Sulfone Trade Names: Thimet, Astar and Rampart	Systemic Organophosphate	Insecticide/nematicide used to control beetles, mites, wireworms, white grubs, aphids, leafminers, thrips, black cutworms, leafhoppers, white flies, psyllids, wireworms, chinch bug nymphs, grasshoppers, and several other pests. Phorate is used on potatoes and other vegetables. In acute or chronic amounts, Phorate can cause cholinesterase inhibition in humans; it can interfere with the nervous system causing nausea, dizziness, confusion, and at very high exposures (e.g., accidents or major spills), respiratory paralysis and death.
Phosmet Trade Names: Appa, Decemthion, Imidan, Kemolate, Fesdan, Prolate, PMC and Safidon	Non-systemic Organophosphate	Phosmet is mainly used on apple trees for control of coddling moth and vines for the control of aphids, suckers, mites and fruit flies. Also used on animals for flea control. It is a mild irritant to eyes and skin. Direct exposure may cause a reduction in enzyme activity (peripheral cholinesterase).
Thiabendazole Trade Names: Benzimidazole, 2-(4-thiazolyl)-; APL-Luster; 4-(2-Benzimidazolyl) thiazole; Eprofil; Thiaben	Benzimidazole	Considered "slightly toxic" by EPA. A fungicide used to control mold, rot, blight, and stain. Also used to treat humans for cutaneous larva migrans (creeping eruption.) Symptoms of acute toxicity include dizziness, anorexia, nausea, and vomiting. In studies with rats, signs of chronic toxicity included a decrease in active bone marrow.

Chapter 14

PESTS & DISEASES

The chart below describes most of the pests and diseases affecting plants grown in traditional gardens. Container gardeners will not experience problems with most of these pests and diseases. Reduction in pests and diseases is a big advantage container gardeners have over traditional gardeners. Follow these few simple rules and you will reduce the risk of pests and diseases even further:

- Begin with healthy soil. Plants are better able to fight off diseases and overcome pest damage when they have all the necessary nutrients they need for growth. I never re-use soil. Soil from spent plants can be spread on the lawn or dumped back into the compost bin.

- Be sure that compost for use in container gardens reaches 105°–145°F during the composting process. This will kill many pests and diseases. Soil with visible destructive pests should be discarded."

- Always use clean containers. Wash used containers with a dilute bleach solution before reusing.

- Keep garden area free of debris and spent produce. Pests like to feed on spoiled food and take shelter under dead plants and weeds.

- Look for pests daily. They can usually be found on plants early in the morning, late in the evening, and just after a rain. Look carefully! Many pests camouflage quite well on stems, leaves and flowers. Remember to look under the leaves and remove any eggs.

- Except during times of pollination, use floating row covers. Many pests hatch in the soil and then fly onto plants to lay eggs. Covering plants prevent the continuation of pests' life cycle. Continue to examine plants for pests even if you use row covers.

- Control moisture. Most diseases affecting container plants are related to moisture levels. Frequently, gardeners over-water plants. Inexpensive moisture meters can be purchased at your local garden center. Remember to dig down below the crust of the soil to check for moisture before watering. If leaves are cupped, the plant usually needs water. If leaves are limp and pointing down, they may have been over-watered.
- Become acquainted with beneficial insects. Encouraging beneficial insects in your garden is like employing your own personal 24 hour bug control service.

Pest Identification, Prevention, & Treatment

PEST	PEST IDENTIFICATION	LIFE CYCLE/ CROP DAMAGE IDENTIFICATION	PREVENTION	ORGANIC TREATMENT
Caterpillars/Moths				
Coddling Moth *Cydia (Laspeyresia) pomonella* Host: Apples	Moth—¼" long. Grayish-red, mottled. Caterpillars—Cream with black head, turn pinkish-brown Eggs on underside of leaves—flat, oval, white. Fig. 14-1: Coddling moth damage inside an apple	Winter as full grown larvae in cocoons under scales of bark. Emerge as adult moths in early spring. Deposit eggs of fruit, leaves, and spurs. Young larvae bore into fruit. After fully developed, larvae drop from fruit onto soil and bark to form cocoons.	Examine trees in fall and early winter and remove cocoons. In early spring, remove eggs.	• Manual Removal • Pheromone traps • Parasitic wasps
Oriental Fruit Moth *(Grapholitha molesta)* Hosts: Peaches, Nectarines	Moth—½" long. Mottled gray at wing base darkens to brown at wingtips. Caterpillars—Yellow with black head to grayish tan with dark brown head. Eggs—on upper side of leaves, oval mass, flattened, green.	Winter as adults in cocoons in protected area of trees or in garden debris at base of tree. Emerge in early spring, laying eggs in terminals. Larvae feed on terminals, shoots, and early maturing fruit.	• Examine trees in fall and early winter and remove cocoons. • In early spring, remove eggs. • Remove caterpillars immediately. • Watch for wilting leaves.	• Manual Removal • Pheromone traps • Parasitic wasps

PEST	PEST IDENTIFICATION	LIFE CYCLE/ CROP DAMAGE IDENTIFICATION	PREVENTION	ORGANIC TREATMENT
Caterpillars/Moths, continued				
Tufted Apple Bud Moth (*Platynota idaeusalis*) Host: Apples	• Moth—½" long. Mottled gray at wing base darkens to brown at wingtips. • Caterpillars—Yellow with black head to grayish tan with dark brown head. • Eggs—on upper side of leaves, oval mass, flattened, green.	Larvae winters in rolled leaves and decayed fruit. 　Moths emerge and lay eggs in May. Feed on and create shelter in leaves. Attach leaves to other leaves and fruit from Spring through summer. Causes increased fruit drop. 　Damage to stem and fruit. Small area of rot where larvae burrow.	Examine trees in fall and early winter and remove cocoons. In early spring, remove eggs. Remove all caterpillars immediately. Watch for curling leaves.	• Manual Removal • Pheromone traps • Parasitic wasps
Grapeberry Moth (*Endopiza vitana Clemens*) Host: Grapes	Moth—⅜" long. Brownish body with gray "saddle" on back. Zigzag flight pattern. Larvae—creamy white with dark brown head. Eggs—opaque, scale-like.	Winters in cocoons in folded leaves and debris on ground. Moths emerge in mid spring and lay eggs on grape flowers. 　Larvae tunnel in fruit, destroying up to 90% of fruit in many vineyards. Damage—red/purple spots on fruit.	Three weeks before flowers bloom, remove all cocoons. Watch for caterpillars in mid May. Watch for webbing in fruit clusters. Watch for zigzagging flight activity in evenings. Remove all caterpillars immediately.	• Manual Removal • Pheromone traps
Cutworms (*Noctuidae Family*) Hosts: Sweet Bell Peppers	Moth—½" long. 1 ½" wingspan. Larvae: 1–2" long. Gray or brown. Eggs—White. Laid on upper surfaces of leaves.	Winter as pupae. Emerge and lay eggs in early summer. Larvae feed on plants for 3–5 weeks. Pupate in soil. Caterpillars feed on stems and young plants at night, often completely cutting the plant in two.	Place stiff cardboard collars around stems of seedlings, pushing collars down into soil. 　Look for eggs and wipe these off leaves with a small amount of dish soap. 　Set out transplants as late in season as possible.	Remove damaged plants and destroy cutworms living in soil beneath plants.

PEST	PEST IDENTIFICATION	LIFE CYCLE/ CROP DAMAGE IDENTIFICATION	PREVENTION	ORGANIC TREATMENT
Beetles				
Plum Curculio Beetle (*Conotrachelus nenuphar*) Hosts: Apples, Peaches, Nectarines	Adult—¼″ long. Dark, brownish gray with warty wings. 4 bumps on back with long snout. Larvae—⅓″ long, fat white grubs with brown heads. Eggs—Round, white, laid under fruit skin.	Adults winter under leaves and debris. Appear in trees when trees blossom. Lay eggs in fruit. Larvae feed in fruit. After fruit drops, larvae move to soil to pupate. Second generation of larvae feeds on fallen fruit. Damage—Crescent shaped cut in fruit's skin followed by fruit drop.	• Always use new soil when planting in containers. • Remove all fallen fruit on a daily basis. • Apply floating row covers before trees blossom.	• Manual removal twice a day throughout growing season • Destroy all fallen fruit. • Apply Pyrethrin and repeat in 7–10 days.
Green June Beetle (*Cotinis nitida L*) Hosts: Peaches, Nectarines	• Adult—¾″ long, ½″ wide. Deep green on top, sometimes with tan stripes. Metallic green or gold underside. Spines on legs. • Grubs—large dirty white grubs with blackish brown heads. Tunnel upside down with legs in air. • Eggs—spherical, white, 1/16″	Winters as a grub, deep in soil. In spring, feeds on decaying matter and roots close to surface of soil. Adults emerge in summer, feeding on foliage and fruit. Damage—stunted, poor plant growth.	Remove any decayed plants and leaves from container garden. Always use new soil when planting and transplanting. Protect pots from grubs by placing copper scrubbing pads or wire mesh in over drainage holes in containers.	• Insecticidal wasps • Pyrethrin • BT • Transplant to new soil
Japanese Beetle (*Popillia japonica*) Hosts: Peaches, Nectarines	Adult—½″ long with metallic green body and bronze wings. © Carolina K Smith M-Fotolia.com **Fig. 14-2: Japanese beetle adult** Grubs—Opaque to white with brown head. 1″ long, lay in curled position. Eggs—White with pointed ends, buried in soil.	Grub winters deep in soil; Feeds on roots in early spring; Grow to maturity and lay eggs in late Spring. Eggs hatch in mid summer and young grubs begin to feed. Damage—adults eat flowers and skeletonize leaves.	Always use new soil when planting and transplanting. Protect pots from grubs by placing copper scrubbing pads or wire mesh in over drainage holes in containers. Use floating row covers.	• Transplant to new soil • Pheromone trap • Parasitic Wasps • Spray plants with Neem

PEST	PEST IDENTIFICATION	LIFE CYCLE/ CROP DAMAGE IDENTIFICATION	PREVENTION	ORGANIC TREATMENT
Beetles, continued				
Colorado Potato Beetle (*Leptinotarsa decemlineata*) Hosts: Potatoes, Tomatoes	Adult—½" long with bright yellow body and 5 brown stripes. Fig. 14-3: Colorado potato beetle Larvae—reddish brown, hump backs, two rows of dark brown spots. Eggs—yellow to orange; laid on underside of leaves in groups of about 30.	Pupate in soil during winter. When temperatures warm, emerge as adults to mate and feed on host plants. Eggs hatch in 4–15 days. Fig. 14-4: Colorado potato beetle larvae	• Inspect for eggs when weather warms. • Manually remove beetles. • Encourage predatory insects by planting pollen and nectar host plants.	• Neem • Pyola
Flea Beetles— Generic name for small, jumping beetles (*Chrysomelidae* Family) Hosts: Spinach, Blueberries	Adult—1/16" long. Elongated/oval shape. Eggs—vary. Laid in soil, on leaves or on edges of holes in leaves.	Adults winter underground or beneath plant debris; Mate and lay eggs in early spring; Larvae develop in summer. Damage—adults feed on the roots, causing stunting of the plant. Skeletonize the leaves.	• Keep container garden free of weeds and debris. • Always use new soil when planting and transplanting. • Plant after soil has warmed (late in season.)	• Cover containerized plants with floating row covers until adults die off. • Change soil in containers. • Move containers to shadier location.
Wireworms or "Click Beetles" (*Limonius* spp.) Host: Potatoes	Adult—⅓" Elongated, hard, light brown, and smooth. Makes a clicking sound when they flip. Larvae—1" long. Yellow to brown. Wire-like. Jointed.	Adults winter in soil. Lay eggs on roots in early spring. Larvae feed on roots. Take up to 6 years to mature. Damage—wireworms feed on seeds, roots, and stems.	It is very unusual for container gardens to suffer damage from wireworms. Always use new soil planting and transplanting. Bury potato pieces 4–6" deep in container.	Check for worms every two days and destroy.

PEST	PEST IDENTIFICATION	LIFE CYCLE/ CROP DAMAGE IDENTIFICATION	PREVENTION	ORGANIC TREATMENT
Stink Bugs				
Green, Brown, & Dusky Stink Bugs (Pentatomidae Family) Hosts: Peaches, Nectarines	Adult—½" long. Adults are distinctly shaped like a shield. Malodorous scent. Fig. 14-5: Stink bug adult Eggs—Masses of white to light yellow eggs on underside of leaves Nymphs—yellowish, red eyes	Winters in tree bark and leaf litter. Lays eggs from spring through winter. Nymphs hatch in 5–10 days, then molts into adult in 8 days. Damage—prefers to suck juice from new growth and fruit, but will eat all parts of plant.	• Keep container garden free of weeds and debris. Always use new soil when planting and transplanting. • Remove eggs from underside of leaves. • Grow small flowering plants in adjacent containers.	• Manual removal • Parasitic wasps • Pyrethrin
Tarnished Plant Bugs (Lygus lineolaris) Hosts: Peaches, Strawberries	Adult—¼" in length. Light brown and spotted white, yellow, and black. Has a tarnished appearance. Yellow triangle with a black dot on the lower third of each side. Nymphs—similar to the adults, but have wing pads instead of wings. Eggs—layed in plant tissue.	Winter under leaf litter and rocks. Feed on early buds of plants. Breed in nearby grasses. Lay eggs on the midrib of leaves and sometimes are inserted into the plant buds. Eggs hatch in 10 days. Damage—Puncture terminal shoot beneath bud, causing plant to wilt and die.	• Keep container garden free of weeds and debris. • Always use new soil when planting and transplanting. • Cover plants with floating row cover.	• Manual removal • Pyrethrin
Maggots/Flies				
Apple Maggot (Rhagoletis pomonella) Host: Apples	Adult—¼" fly. Yellow legs. Transparent wings with dark bands. Larvae—¼" maggot.	Pupae winter in soil. Adults emerge in mid summer and lay eggs in fruit. Damage—fruit drop due to larvae tunneling.	• Always start with new soil. • Destroy all dropped fruit daily. • Grow late maturing varieties.	Hang apple maggot traps in trees from summer through harvest.

PEST	PEST IDENTIFICATION	LIFE CYCLE/ CROP DAMAGE IDENTIFICATION	PREVENTION	ORGANIC TREATMENT
Cherry Maggot (*Rhagoletis cingulata*) Host: Cherries	Adult—⅛" long. Yellow legs. Transparent wings with dark bands. Cream colored spot in center of the back. Larvae—¼" long. Glossy white. Legless. Eggs—Oval, white; Layed in fruit.	Pupae winter in soil; adults emerge in late spring and feed on leaves and fruit for 10 days before laying eggs in fruit. Maggots hatch in 5 days and feed on fruit, then drop to the ground and burrow in soil. Damage—infested fruit.	• Always start with new soil. • Use floating row covers.	Red Sticky Spheres (traps)
Other Pests				
Mites (*Panonychus ulmi*) Hosts: Apples, Grapes	Adults—tiny, red. Eggs—winter on trees.	Winter on plants; Suck juice from leaves; Leave yellow speckles. Damage to leaves decreases chlorophyll production.	Other than spraying the plants with strong streams of water, there is not much that can be done to prevent mites.	• Try spraying mites off plants with water • Insecticidal soap • Lime-sulfur spray early in season
Aphids Also called Blackfly, Greenfly, or Wooly Aphids (*Aphididae* Family) Hosts: Peaches, Nectarines, Cherries, Lettuce, Kale	Adults—⅛" long, Pear-shaped. 2 short tubes project backward from abdomen. Long antennae. Wings. **Fig. 14-6: Aphid adults** Nymphs—similar to adults	Eggs winter on stems. Hatch into females in spring; Do not have to mate to reproduce. Males and females are born in fall. These mate to produce eggs for wintering. Damage to leaf buds and flowers due to sucking of plant juices. Leaves and flowers may drop. Fruit is stunted. Secrete honeydew and are often farmed by ants.	• Plant pollen and nectar plants to attract natural predators. • Routinely spray plants with strong stream of water.	• Try spraying with a strong stream of water. • Place containers in moat of water to discourage ants. • Release lady beetles • Spray with insecticidal soap • Fruit trees—spray with dormant oil. • Pyrethrin

PEST	PEST IDENTIFICATION	LIFE CYCLE/ CROP DAMAGE IDENTIFICATION	PREVENTION	ORGANIC TREATMENT
Other Pests, continued				
Chinch Bugs (*Blissus leucopterus*) Hosts: Peaches, Nectarines	Adults—1/16" long. Gray with white forewings and black triangular spot near outer edges of wings. Nymphs—⅛" long. Young nymphs are bright red with a white stripe on back. Older nymphs are dark gray with white spots in middle of back.	Adults winter in grass on fence rows and areas not mowed routinely. Lay eggs on roots. Nymphs emerge in 1–3 weeks and food on roots. Molt into adults in summer. Damage—Sap sucked from roots and stems. Plants yellow and die.	Container gardens do not usually experience problems with Chinch bugs. Avoid placing containers on grass where chinch bugs have been identified.	Spray affected plants with soapy water.
Thrips (*Thripidae* Family) Hosts: Peaches, Nectarines	Adults—tiny and thin. Yellow, brown or black. Fast moving—leap and fly when plants are disturbed. Nymphs—Light green, yellow. Appearance is similar to adults.	Adults winter in soil, plant debris, and loose bark. Lay eggs in plant tissue in spring. Nymphs feed for 2 weeks, then rest and molt in soil or on leaves. Damage—Adults and Nymphs suck plant juices. Leave silver streaks on leaves. Stunts plants and damages fruits and flowers.	• Always begin with new soil. • Keep container garden area clean of debris.	• Dust bottom of leaves with Diatomaceous earth. • Fruit trees: spray with dormant oil. • Release lady beetles. • Insecticidal soap • Pyrethrin
Leafhoppers (*Cicadellidae*) Hosts: Lettuce, celery, tomato, sweet bell peppers	Adults—1/10" long, green or brown. Wedge shaped. Slender. Jump quickly when plants are disturbed. **Fig. 14-7: Leafhopper adult** Nymphs—Similar in appearance to adults except pale and wingless.	Adults winter in the south and migrate north to lay eggs in summer. Eggs are laid in leaves and stems. Hatch 2 weeks later. Damage—suck juice from leaves. Toxic saliva causes stunting, tip-burn, and yellow curled leaves. White spots are often visible on underside of leaves.	Spray plants with water frequently to discourage leafhoppers from taking up residence on containerized plants.	• Insecticidal soap • Neem • Pyrethrin

PEST	PEST IDENTIFICATION	LIFE CYCLE/ CROP DAMAGE IDENTIFICATION	PREVENTION	ORGANIC TREATMENT
Other Pests, continued				
Leafminers (*Agromyzidae* Family) Host: Spinach	Adult Flies—1/10″ long. Black, sometimes with yellow. Larvae—Pale green to translucent maggots. Eggs—laid in clusters under leaves. White. Cylindrical.	Cocoon in winter. Adults emerge in spring. Lay eggs on leaves. Larvae tunnel in leaves and then drop to soil to pupate. Damage—Tunneling often causes young plants to die.	• Always begin with new soil. • Use floating row covers.	• Remove egg clusters from bottom of leaves with a paper towel and small drop of dish soap. • Plant nectar plants nearby • Neem
Pear Psylla (*Cacopsylla pyricola*) Hosts: Pears	Adults—8/100″–11/100″ long. Light orange to red brown with 4 dark stripes on back. Nymphs: yellow graduating to brown with age. Similar to aphids in appearance. Eggs: cream-yellowish orange. Elliptical with tiny peg inserted in plant tissue.	Adults winter in pear orchards. Mate in spring, laying eggs on fruit spurs and young leaves. Nymphs accumulate in drops of honeydew. Honeydew serves as growth medium for mold and causes black russet on fruit.	• Select resistant cultivars. Pear decline occurs on European scions grown on Asian rootstocks. • Hang yellow sticky traps to monitor for eggs. • Shake tree limbs while holding a tray beneath limb. Look for adults on tray.	Dormant oil may be applied when eggs are observed in spring.
Mollusks— Slugs & Snails Hosts: Strawberries, lettuce	Adults—⅛″–8″ long. Usually gray, black, yellow, or green. Slugs have no shells. Snails have coiled shells. Eggs—clear, oval, laid encapsulated in jelly under garden debris and in cracks in soil.	After eggs hatch, mollusks travel in the soil, damaging root crops and germinating seeds. Slugs can travel into plant containers through drainage holes. Damage—Slugs emerge from soil at night to feed on plant material. Also feed on maturing fruits and vegetables. This creates wounds that allow bacteria and fungi to destroy the harvest.	• Remove all garden debris from the container garden. • Place copper scrubbing pads over drainage holes in containers before planting. • Place a copper "collar" around perimeter of container at base.	• Bury a small cup of beer to soil level. This will trap slugs. • Place board on ground at night and turn over in the morning. Destroy all slugs that have gathered for shelter. • Sprinkle soil with diatomaceous earth.

PEST	PEST IDENTIFICATION	LIFE CYCLE/ CROP DAMAGE IDENTIFICATION	PREVENTION	ORGANIC TREATMENT
Other Pests, continued				
Yellow Jackets (*Vespula spp.*) Host: Grapes	Adults—½" long. Yellow and black striped abdomens. Two pair of wings. Larvae—white grubs.	Yellow jackets are wasps and are usually thought to be beneficial in garden. However, in late autumn, they transition from eating insects to eating sugary plants and fruits.	Harvest grapes as soon as they ripen. Remove all spoiled fruit.	No effective treatment.
Rabbits, Deer, Birds Hosts: **Rabbits**— Tomatoes, Potatoes, Sweet Bell Peppers **Deer**— Lettuce, Grapes, Berries, Tomatoes, Fruit trees **Birds**— Strawberries, Cherries, Grapes, Blueberry			• Rabbits—erect chicken wire fence around garden. • Deer—Electric fence. I don't have problems with deer if my dogs frequent the garden. They seem to be deterred by the dogs' scent. • Birds—Use netting or lose your strawberry crop.	• Ask your local veterinarian about humane pet traps. Be aware, however, that wild rabbits die very quickly from fright. • Bar soap, eggs and water poured on the garden soil, and human hair are all said to help repel deer. • Experiment with motion detectors. Some can trigger a spray of water or loud noise to scare off animals.

Disease Identification, Prevention, & Treatment

DISEASE	DESCRIPTION	CROP DAMAGE IDENTIFICATION	PREVENTION	TREATMENT
Anthracnose (Rust) Hosts: Peppers, Grapes, Spinach	Fungal disease affecting fruit.	Small, dark spots, sometimes with pink spores in middle. Can spread, causing fruit to rot.	• Plant resistant cultivars. • Move container location each year.	• Copper Spray • Destroy infected plants.
Cedar-Apple Rust Host: Apples	Fungal infection caused by close proximity of cedar and apple trees.	Yellow spots appear in spring. Turn orange on leaves and fruit. Underside of leaves have brown spots.	• Do not plant apple trees within 4 miles of cedar trees. • Keep trees leaves as dry as possible.	• Sulfur • Lime sulfur • Copper-based fungicide.
Powdery Mildew (*Podosphaera leucotricha*) Hosts: Apples, Grapes, Spinach	Fungal disease. Spread by spores in areas of high humidity. Spores are spread by wind and winter in plant debris.	Dusty white coating on leaf and other plant surfaces. Causes tissue death, plant stunting, distortion of plant tissues and fruit and premature leaf drop.	• Plant mildew resistant varieties. • Ensure good air circulation to all parts of the plant. • Expose plant to direct sunlight.	• Pick off affected leaves and destroy. • Spray leaves with baking soda: 1 teaspoon soda to 1 quart water. • Some gardeners have success slowing the disease by spraying a solution of 1 part cows milk with 9 parts water.[29]
Black Rot (*Alternaria radicina*) Hosts: Apples, Grapes	Fungus spread by spores in conditions of high precipitation and high temperatures. Most commonly found in Coastal Mountain Valleys.	Weakens leaves and causes fruit rot, starting at the top of the fruit.	• Place strawberry plant containers in an area protected from excess moisture. • Plant only certified disease free plants and seeds.	Remove diseased fruit and move plants to a location protected from moisture.
Brown Rot (*Monilinia laxa* and *Monilinia fructicola*) Hosts: Apples, Pears	Fungus spread by spores in conditions of high precipitation and temperatures in the mid-seventies (F.)	Blossom and twig blight causes death to young blossom spurs and leaves. A sap-like exudate is often present at the base of flowers.	• Remove and destroy all fruit "mummies" and blighted shoots. • Remove all garden debris each season.	Remove diseased fruit and move plants to a location protected from moisture.

---

29. "Powdery Mildew: Steps to Prevention," http://organicgardening.com/learn-and-grow/powdery-mildew

DISEASE	DESCRIPTION	CROP DAMAGE IDENTIFICATION	PREVENTION	TREATMENT
Rhizopus Fruit Rot Host: Strawberries	Fungal disease affecting strawberries. Spread during periods of high humidity. Spores travel through the air.	Initially appears as water soaked spots on fruit. Spots enlarge, causing fruit to turn brown and leak juice.	• Remove all ripe fruit from containers. • When harvesting, remove entire fruit from stem. • Plant resistant varieties. • Cool fruit to 46°F immediately after harvesting.	No effective treatment.
Scab (*Spilocaea and Venturia spp.*) Host: Apple Trees	Fungal disease causing scabby, sunken spots of fruit and resulting in dropped fruit and sometimes death of shoots.	Winters infected garden debris and sometimes on lesions on live plants. Spores spread by rain or irrigation in spring. Primarily spread in spring during periods of mild temperatures and high humidity.	• Remove garden debris in fall. • Avoid overhead irrigation. • Apply sulfur to foliage weekly during wet periods.	Treatment is impractical.
Wilt Fusarium and Verticulum Host: Spinach	Caused by a fungi. Generally enters plant through roots and grows up through water conducting vessels. Blocks water supply to leaves, causing plants to wilt. Especially affects heirloom tomatoes and peppers, strawberries, and potatoes.	Fusarium—Causes yellowing and death of leaves on one side of stem. Dark reddish, brown lines appear on stem. Verticulum—Causes V-shaped yellowing on leaves. Tan lines appear on stem.	• Always begin with new soil. • Move containers to new location each growing season. • Remove all garden debris each season. • Destroy any infested plants. • Maintain plants to ensure vigor. • Plant disease resistant varieties.	Destroy all infested plant material to discourage spread of the disease.
Bacterial Spot	Bacterial disease affecting woody and herbaceous plants.	Long brown discoloration on leaf caused by bacteria. Spots may have a yellow halo around them. On fruit, bacteria leave sunken areas.	• Use clean seeds and new soil. • Remove all garden debris. • Plant resistant cultivars.	• Remove all infested plants. • Copper Spray

DISEASE	DESCRIPTION	CROP DAMAGE IDENTIFICATION	PREVENTION	TREATMENT
Canker	Bacterial condition. Kills plant cells.	Kills plant cells, creating sunken areas. Creates slimy ooze. Circle around plant stems and trunks. Everything above the canker wilts and dies.	Always wash pruners in dilute bleach solution after use.	• Prune infected plant parts. • Copper compounds are mildly effective.
Celery Mosaic Host: Celery	Viral disease vectored by aphids.	Foliage turns yellow. Mottling patterns appear on leaves. Crinkled and distorted foliage. Necrotic leaf spots develop on older foliage. Sometimes plants become stunted.	Remove all weeds and garden debris from garden area.	If virus is discovered, prevent further spread by destroying plants and waiting 2–3 months before replanting.
Pear Blight (*Erwinia amylovora*) Hosts: Pears, Apples	Bacterial condition affecting all parts of pear and sometimes apple trees. Millions of bacteria are transmitted through a sticky ooze to plant tissues. Spread through rain splash and insects.	Tissue wilts, blackens, and dies. Tree can die when disease moves into the trunk, roots, and main limbs of the tree.	• Remove any canker branches. These are often the wintering place for Pear Blight bacteria. • Sterilize pruning shears after each use.	• Place containers in areas protected from rain. • Copper spray
Prunus Stem Pitting Virus Hosts: Stone fruit (cherries, peaches, nectarines)	Viral disease affecting stone fruit. Associated with tomato ringspot virus. Transmitted by to trees by nematodes via weeds, including dandelions. Can attack all stone fruit species.	Causes pits to swell. Lower bark and sapwood thickens. Roots develop poorly. Trunk girdling.	Only purchase certified virus-free trees.	Currently, there is no effective monitoring or treatment program.
Plum Pox Virus (PPV) Hosts: Stone fruit (cherries, peaches, nectarines)	Viral disease affecting stone fruit. Spread by Aphids.	Found mostly in the North East U.S., Europe, and South America. Causes ringspots on fruit and leaves and eventually causes tree to be non-productive.	• Only purchase certified virus-free trees. • Control aphid populations.	Destroy infected trees immediately.

DISEASE	DESCRIPTION	CROP DAMAGE IDENTIFICATION	PREVENTION	TREATMENT
Leaf Curl Hosts: tomatoes, peppers, potatoes	Viral disease affecting tomatoes and peppers. Spread by Sweet Potato whiteflies and leafhoppers. Also spread by movement of infected plants. Found primarily in southern U.S.	Causes shortened stems and small, curled leaves that turn upward. Leaves will yellow outer margins, flower drop and drastically reduced production.	• Select resistant varieties. • Control whiteflies. • Do not import tomatoes from infected states—Florida, Georgia, Texas, & Mexico. • Use floating row covers. • Control weeds. Remove all garden debris each season.	No effective treatment. Some research indicates effectiveness with UV blocking plastic shields.[30]

X-Disease
 	
Hosts: cherries, peaches, nectarines
	Mycoplasma disease affecting peaches nectarines, and cherries.
	    Transmitted by leafhoppers that have fed on chokecherries.
		Inward curling leaves with irregular, yellow to purplish spots. Spotted portions of leaves fall out, leaving holes and tattered appearance on leaves. Premature leaf drop starts at the base of the branch and eventually leaves only a few leaves at the top of the branch.
		    In cherries, trees can die suddenly depending on the rootstock.
		    Fruit is small, pink, and bitter.
			• Do not place containers near chokecherries.
			• Control leafhopper population.
			• Do not place young peach trees near old cherry trees.
				No effective treatment.

---

30. F. Monci, et al, "Tomato Yellow Leaf Curl Disease Control With UV-Blocking Plastic Covers in Commercial Plastic Houses of Southern Spain," *Acta Hort.* (International Society for Horticulture Science) (2004) 633:537-542, http://www.actahort.org/books/633/633_68.htm

Common Nutrient Deficiencies in Vegetable & Fruit Plants[31]

Nutrient	Description of Nutrient	Appearance in Deficient Plant	Organic Amendment
Nitrogen	Necessary for photosynthesis, cell growth, and reproduction. Element plants use in greatest amounts.	Varies in each plant. Usually causes yellowing and poor growth.	For proper soil nitrification:[32] • Add organic matter such as aged manure, cottonseed, and composted plant materials to soil. • Maintain pH of 5.8–7.0 • Garden in temperatures over 50°F • Keep soil adequately aerated. • Maintain adequate moisture in soil.
Phosphorous	Required for cell growth, plant reproduction, flower and fruit formation.	Undersized growth; dark green leaves change to purple on undersides. In final stages, leaves yellow. Poor flowering and fruiting. Occurs mostly in cold, wet, and acidic soil.	• Maintain pH above 5.0. • Amend with bone meal or rock phosphate.
Potassium	Necessary for formation of flowers, leaves, and fruit. Necessary for photosynthesis in low light conditions and plants' water regulation. Increases plant resistance to stress including insect, disease, and frost. Improves flavor of crops.	Occurs in sandy and acidic soils.	Amend with kelp and seaweed.
Calcium	Strengthens stems and other plant parts.	Yellow, then browning of young leaves. Blossom end rot in tomatoes and tip-burn in lettuce.	Amend with eggshells and oystershells.

---

31. cf "Interpretive/Recommendation Statements for Nutrients," Rutgers Soil Testing Laboratory. New Jersey Agriculture Experiment Station.

32. J. M. Stephens, S. R. Kostewicz, "Producing Garden Vegetables with Organic Soil Amendments," University of Florida IFAS Extension, http://edis.ifas.ufl.edu/pdffiles/MG/MG32300.pdf

Nutrient	Description of Nutrient	Appearance in Deficient Plant	Organic Amendment
Magnesium	Necessary in photosynthesis. Aids in action of nitrogen, phosphorus and sulfur. Aids in cleansing plant of natural toxins developed by plants metabolism. Assists in the formation of proteins.	First symptoms include discoloring of veins in lower leaves. Leaves become thin and brittle and may cup upward.	• Epsom salts • Fishmeal • Greensand
Iron	Needed for formation of chlorophyll. Aids in oxidization of sugar for energy; Plays a role in regulating respiration of plant's cells.	Symptoms look the same as Magnesium deficiency. Occurs mostly in alkaline soils with excess phosphorous. Yellow leaves with green veins. Yellowing begins at top of plant and moves down. Shoots may die back and fruit may be discolored.	• Correct pH to 7.0. • Add bone meal or blood organic meal.
Zinc	Needed for stem growth and formation of flowers.	Appearance similar to Nitrogen deficiency. Young leaves often small, yellow, and deformed.	• Maintain soil pH of 5.8–6.2. • Apply aged organic manure.
Boron	Involved in movement of sugar within plant; Necessary for cell division, flower formation and pollination.	• Rust colored cracks in stems and leaf stalks. • Thick, leathery leaves. • No flower bloom. New growth dies back.	• Borax • Maintain soil pH at 7.0
Copper	Necessary for photosynthesis, plant respiration, and iron uptake. Occurs most commonly in peat-based soils.	Small leaves with brown spots near the tips of leaves. Rosetting of the leaves and damage or death to terminal shoots.	• Amend with composted leaf matter. • Do not over-fertilize with lime or phosphorous.

Raised Growing Beds

If you have an in-ground garden, increase your yield per square foot by building raised growing beds. Treat them like large containers. If your existing soil is not so good, fill the beds with the same ideal soil mix that you would use in containers. Close spacing and succession planting (putting in another planting as soon as space opens up) will result in abundant harvests from a small amount of space.

Raised growing beds.
Beds with cedar wood sides in the foreground and without sides in the background.

Building Raised Beds

Before building beds, spread any compost or other fertilizers. Till or spade the garden deeply. The soil should be somewhat dry for this. You should be able to squeeze a handful and have it break when dropped.

Mark bed edges with strings or hoses. About 3′–4′ (1–1.25 meters) is the usual bed width. You should be able to reach the middle. You may want paths wide enough for a garden cart.

If the existing soil is good, you can dig some from the paths and toss on beds until they are 3″–8″ (8–20 cm) higher than paths. You can install plastic, wood, or brick sides. This makes it easier to use weed guard fabric in the paths, covered by wood chips, stones, or patio blocks. Wood sides should be untreated. A rot resistant type such as cedar will last longer.

Beds without sides sometimes need re-shaping. Make a flat-topped bed with sloping sides or a low arch gradually sloping to the path.

The idea with raised beds is to walk on paths; never on the beds. The lack of compaction, combined with mulching, compost, and earthworm activity, will eventually create fertile, easily worked soil.

Raised growing bed with lettuce

Selected Resources/Bibliography

This is not an exhaustive list. I have not personally dealt with all of the companies listed, so inclusion here does not necessarily represent an endorsement. Visit **www.containergardeningforhealth.com** for more resources and updates.

Sources for Seeds, Plants, Books, & Gardening Supplies

Company or Organization	Address/Phone	Products Available
Gourmet Gardener www.gourmetgardener.com gginfo@windstream.net	12287 117 Drive Live Oak FL 32060 386-362-9089 Fax: 407-650-2691	Organic vegetable seeds & plants. Fruit trees & plants. Containers, cover crops, tools, gift certificates, online classes, books. Several varieties of each of the Dirty Dozen.
Prairie Oak Publishing www.PrairieOakPublishing.com prairieoakpub@gmail.com	221 S. Saunders St. Maryville MO 64468 660-528-0768 Fax: 866-790-3987	Publisher of *Organic Container Gardening, Growing & Using Stevia,* and other books. Inquire about wholesale purchasing.
The Arbor Day Foundation www.arborday.org	100 Arbor Avenue Nebraska City, NE 68410 888-448-7337	Fruit trees. Discounted prices for members.
Baker Creek Heirloom Seeds http://rareseeds.com	2278 Baker Creek Rd. Mansfield MO 65704 417-924-8917	Heirloom vegetable seeds including cutting celery, New Zealand & Malabar spinach.
Bountiful Gardens www.bountifulgardens.org	18001 Shafer Ranch Rd Willits CA 95490 707-459-6410	Heirloom vegetable seeds including cutting celery, New Zealand & Malabar spinach.
Gardens Alive www.gardensalive.com	5100 Schenley Place Lawrenceburg IN 47025 513-354-1482	Specializes in organic pest & disease control. Also fruit trees, berry plants, & vegetable seeds.
High Mowing Organic Seeds www.highmowingseeds.com	76 Quarry Road Wolcott VT 05680 802-472-6174	Organic vegetable seeds, organic growing supplies
Ison's Nursery www.isons.com	P.O. Box 190 Brooks, GA 30205 800-733-0324	Fruit trees & muscadine grapes
Johnny's Selected Seeds www.johnnyseeds.com	955 Benton Ave Winslow ME 04901 877-564-6697	Organic vegetable seeds including Malabar spinach, cutting celery, Strawberry seeds, plants, supplies.

J. W. Jung Seed Company www.jungseed.com	335 S. High St. Randolph WI 53957 800-247-5864	Vegetable seeds, fruit trees & plants, growing supplies
Miller Nurseries www.millernurseries.com	5060 West Lake Rd. Canandaigua NY 14424 800-836-9630	Fruit trees, berries, & grapes, especially for colder climates
Morgan County Seeds www.morgancountyseeds.com	18761 Kelsay Rd. Barnett MO 65011 573-378-2655	Organic vegetable seeds, organic growing supplies
Mountain Valley Growers www.mountainvalleygrowers.com	38325 Pepperweed Rd Squaw Valley CA 93675	Organic plants, organic gardening Supplies
Nature Hills Nursery www.naturehills.com	3334 N 88 Plaza Omaha NE 68134	Organic fruit trees & plants, organic growing supplies
Peaceful Valley Farm & Garden Supply www.groworganic.com	125 Clydesdale Court Grass Valley CA 95945 888-784-1722	Organic vegetable seeds, fruit trees & plants, organic growing supplies
Pinetree Garden Seeds www.superseeds.com	PO BOX 300, New Gloucester ME 04260 207-926-3400	Vegetable & strawberry seeds, growing supplies
Raintree Nursery www.raintreenursery.com	391 Butts Road Morton, WA 98356 360-496-6400	Fruit trees & plants
Seedman.com www.seedman.com	3421 Bream St. Gautier MS 39553	Vegetable & strawberry seeds, seed starting supplies
Seed Savers Exchange www.seedsavers.org	3094 N Winn Rd. Decorah IA 52101 563-382-5990	Organic vegetable seeds
Seeds of Change www.seedsofchange.com	888-762-7333	Organic heirloom seeds, fruit trees, plants, growing supplies
Southern Exposure Seed Exchange www.southernexposure.com	P.O. Box 460 Mineral VA 23117 540-894-9480	Organic vegetable seeds, organic growing supplies
Territorial Seed Company www.territorialseed.com	PO Box 158 Cottage Grove OR 97424 800-626-0866	Vegetable seeds, fruit trees, & berry plants.
Totally Tomatoes www.totallytomato.com	334 W Stroud Street Randolph, WI 53956 800-345-5977	Tomatoes and peppers including varieties suitable for container gardening
Trees of Antiquity www.treesofantiquity.com,	20 Wellsona Road Paso Robles CA 93446 805-467-9909	Organic heirloom fruit trees

Selected Resources

Visual Gallery of Images of Tree Fruit Insect Pests in the Mid-Atlantic Region
  www.caf.wvu.edu/kearneysville/wvufarm14.html
  West Virginia University, Kearneysville Tree Fruit Research & Education Center

Visual Gallery of Images of Tree Fruit Diseases in the Mid-Atlantic Region
  www.caf.wvu.edu/kearneysville/wvufarm11.html
  West Virginia University, Kearneysville Tree Fruit Research & Education Center

Fruit Pathology Resources at The Ohio State University
  http://www.oardc.ohio-state.edu/fruitpathology/
  Ohio State University, Ohio Agricultural Research & Development Center

Fact Sheets
  http://www.clemson.edu/extension/hgic/
  Clemson Extension Home & Garden Information Center

Training & Pruning Fruit Trees
  www.ces.ncsu.edu/depts/hort/hil/ag29.html
  North Carolina Cooperative Extension Service

Growing Pears in Florida. T.E. Crocker & W.B. Sherman
  http://dixie.ifas.ufl.edu/pdfs/gardening/pear.pdf
  Florida Cooperative Extension Service, Circular 343, March 1994.

Vegetable Varieties for Gardeners
  http://vegvariety.cce.cornell.edu
  Cornell's College of Agriculture and Life Sciences.
  Ranks vegetables for taste, yield, ease of growing, and other criteria.

Producing Garden Vegetables with Organic Soil Amendments
  http://edis.ifas.ufl.edu/MG323
  J. M. Stephens, S. R. Kostewicz. University of Florida IFAS Extension

Recommended Books

Apples and Man
  Fred Lape (New York: Van Nostrand Reinhold, 1979)
  About the history of apples

The Organic Gardener's Handbook of Natural Insect and Disease Control
  Barbara W. Ellis and Fen Marshall Bradley (Emmaus, PA: Rodale Press, 1992)

The Garden Primer
  Barbara Damrosch (Workman Publishing, 1988)

Glossary

beneficial insects—Insects that perform valuable functions like pollination or pest control.

bolting—In the plant world, this means blossoming and seed production. Bolting signals the end of leaf harvest for crops like spinach.

bottom watering—Any watering method that allows the soil to soak up water from below, avoiding wet leaves. In container gardening, this is usually done by placing pots in a shallow container of water.

BT—Bacillus thuringiensis. A microbial organism that controls caterpillar pests when sprayed on plants.

bud union—The point where a plant (usually a tree) has been bud grafted, usually forming a swollen spot. The bud union should not be buried when planting.

Center for Food Safety and Applied Nutrition—One of six centers within the FDA (www.cfsan.fda.gov/list.html). Produced the *Total Diet Study* (TDS) quantifying the cumulative and combined levels of pesticides fed to children.

chemical—A substance having a uniform elemental composition that cannot be separated into other substances without employing a chemical reaction. Technically, this includes common substances such as pure water, sodium chloride (salt), and sucrose (sugar). The term "chemical" is sometimes used as a shorthand term for man-made chemicals not approved for use in organic crop production.

chill hours—The cold winter hours necessary to triggering blossoming in some plants, especially peaches, nectarines, and apples.

compost—Decomposed organic matter used as a soil amendment or an ingredient in potting soil. Improves soil structure and fertility. A good compost pile will heat up thanks to the decomposition process. The heat will kill many destructive diseases and pests.

Consumers Union—A nonprofit testing organization serving consumers (www.consumersunion.org/about/).

copper scrubbing pads—A cleaning tool made of coppers strands, but also useful for placing over container drainage holes to exclude pests.

copper spray—Organic sprays with copper are often used as fungicides.

diatomaceous earth—Ground fossils of prehistoric diatoms. An organic control for soft-bodied pests.

dirty dozen—A nickname coined by the Environmental Working Group for their list of the 12 fruits and vegetables found to contain the most pesticide residues (www.foodnews.org/).

dolomite lime—A slow-acting, naturally

occurring fertilizer. A valuable source of calcium and magnesium. Also raises soil pH.

dormant—Resting. Temporarily less active. Many plants go dormant in the winter season.

dormant oil—A spray designed for pest control, applied to trees while they are dormant.

dwarf fruit tree—A tree kept smaller than normal, usually by grafting the desired variety to a dwarfing rootstock.

elemental sulfur—A soil amendment often used to lower soil pH.

Environmental Working Group (EWG)—A nonprofit environmental research organization. Based on an analysis of FDA data, they compiled the "Dirty Dozen" list—the top 12 most contaminated fruits and vegetables (www.ewg.org/about).

EPA—U.S. Environmental Protection Agency

espalier—Training and pruning trees or vines to create a flat plane on a wall, fence, or trellis.

EWG—Environmental Working Group

FDA—U.S. Food and Drug Administration. A government regulatory agency.

fish emulsion—Fish-based fertilizer rich in nitrogen, phosphorous, potassium, and micronutrients.

floating row covers—A very lightweight fabric designed to be placed directly over plants, protecting them from frost and many pests while allowing air, water, and sunlight to pass through to the plant.

grafting—Asexual propagation by fusing plant tissues in various ways. A given variety is grafted on a rootstock which imparts desirable growth characteristics.

graft union—The point where a plant (usually a tree) has been grafted, usually forming a swollen spot. The graft union should not be buried when planting.

greensand—A slow-release natural fertilizer formed in marine deposits. Supplies mainly potassium (potash) and many other trace minerals. It can be used in potting soil, as a garden soil conditioner, or as a top dressing.

growing on—Plant growth coming after the seedling stage.

heading cut—Removing the tip of a branch to force formation of side branches.

heirloom varieties—Plant varieties that were grown during earlier periods of history, but are not commonly grown on a large commercial scale today. Many are unsuitable for long-distance shipping, but have traits making them valuable for the home garden.

insecticidal soap—Soap-based liquid designed to control certain soft bodied pests such as aphids by a direct spray application.

kelp—Seaweed used to make a fertilizer rich in many valuable nutrients. Available as a liquid or powder.

lady beetle—A beneficial insect, also known as lady bug, that feeds on pests such as aphids.

lateral branches—Side branches that grow directly from a main branch or stem.

leader—The main, leading shoot. On a young fruit tree, there is only one leader and it usually grows straight up.

lime-sulfur spray—A fungicide used on many fruit crops. Also used for control of some insect pests.

loam—Soil with a fairly balanced composition of sand, silt, and clay. Desirable for most garden plants.

National Research Council—"Part of a private, nonprofit institution that provides science, technology and health policy advice under a congressional charter" (http://sites.nationalacademies.org/nrc/index.htm).

neem—A tree native to India. An organic insecticide is made from neem seed oil.

organic foods—Foods grown without the use of certain artificial pesticides, fertilizers, and other inputs specified by the government or certifying agencies.

organic matter— Plant and animal material that has decayed. Vital for optimum soil structure and fertility. Can be supplied by mulching with organic materials or incorporating compost into the soil.

parasitic wasps—Small wasps that parasitize larvae of other insects. Certain species are available for purchase as a control for some insect pests.

peat moss—A natural, organic soil conditioner consisting of partially decayed mosses.

perennial plant— A plant species that normally lives more than two growing seasons.

perlite— A type of volcanic glass. Horticultural perlite is very lightweight. It has been expanded and has the appearance of small white beads. It adds air spaces to potting and seed starting mixes.

pesticide—A substance or mixture for controlling unwanted living organisms such as certain insects, weeds, and diseases. "Under United States law, a pesticide is also any substance or mixture of substances intended for use as a plant regulator, defoliant, or desiccant" (http://www.epa.gov/opp00001/about/).

pH—A measure of acidity or alkalinity. Seven on the pH scale is neutral. Below seven is acid, and above seven is alkaline. Different plants have differing preferences for soil pH range.

pollination—The transfer of pollen in flowering plants. Pollen may be carried by agents such as wind or insects.

pruning—Removing unwanted portions from a plant. Especially needed for most fruit trees.

pyrethrins—Insecticides derived from the pyrethrum plant, a type of chrysanthemum.

rock phosphate—Rock with a high proportion of phosphate minerals. Phosphate is one of the macro-nutrients needed by plants and may be supplied by fertilizers derived from rock phosphate.

rootstock—An established plant that provides the root system for a variety grafted to it. For dwarf fruit trees, it is the rootstock that controls tree size and some of the other characteristics.

self-fertile—Capable of self fertilization.

A self-fertile plant variety does not need pollen from a different variety in order to produce fruit.

thinning cut—Cutting a branch at the point where it originates on another branch or on the trunk, removing the branch entirely.

tobacco mosaic virus—Plant disease affecting peppers, tomatoes, tobacco, and many more species. Produces a mosaic-like coloration on leaves. Can be transmitted by smoking and then handling plants.

top dressing—Applying fertilizer on top of the ground next to a plant.

Total Diet Study—A study prepared by the FDA and Center for Food Safety and Applied Nutrition considering pesticide residue levels on commonly eaten foods. Also known as the *Market Basket Study* (www.cfsan.fda.gov/ ~comm/tds-toc.html).

USDA—U.S. Department of Agriculture

USDA Plant Hardiness Zone—Revised in 1990, the USDA "Plant Hardiness Zone Map" divides the U.S. into 11 zones based on "average annual minimum temperatures" (http://www.usna.usda.gov/Hardzone/).

vector— An organism, usually an insect, that transmits a disease from one place to another, such as between plants.

vermiculite— A natural mineral with a high cation exchange capacity. Horticultural vermiculite has been expanded and is very lightweight. It also improves soil drainage.

Index

A
Agency for Toxic Substances and Disease Registry (ATSDR) – 11
anthracnose (rust) – 45, 50, 57, 62, **99**
aphids – 69, 78, 80, 82, **95**
apple maggot – 94
apples – 15–22

B
bacillus thuringiensis – 81, 92
bacterial spot – 45, 100
baking soda treatment – 82
bell peppers – 59–63
beneficial insects – 90–95
birds – 73, 98
black rot – 20, 99
blueberry – 71–73
blueberry gall midge – 73
blueberry stem blight – 73
bolting – 26, 50
bone meal – 103, 104
boron – 25, **104**
botrytis (head rot) – 73, 82
bottom watering – 80, 62
brown rot – 45, 84, **99**
brussels sprouts – 79
BT—Bacillus thuringiensis – 81, 92
bud union – 44

C
cabbage worms – 81
cabbage loopers – 81
canker – 45, 101
cedar-apple rust – 20, **99**
celery – 23–27
celery mosaic – 26, **101**

Center for Food Safety and Applied Nutrition – 12
chemical residue – see "pesticide residue"
cherry maggot – 95
chill hours
    for apples – 17
    for peaches – 40, 41, 42
chinch bugs – 96
chitting – 68
club root – 82
coddling moth – 16, 20, **90**
collards – 79
compost – 72, 103, 104, 105
composted manure – 25, 35, 52
Consumers Union – 15
containers for growing – 10
    for apples – 19
    for blueberry – 72
    for celery – 25
    for grapes – 55
    for kale – 80
    for lettuce – 77
    for peaches & nectarines – 42
    for peppers – 61–66
    for potatoes – 67–68
    for spinach – 49
    for strawberries – 32–34
Colorado potato beetle – 69, **93**
Colorado potato beetle larvae – 93
copper scrubbing pads – 19, 92. 97
copper spray – 99, 100, 101
caterpillars – 73, 26, 50, 73, 81, 90, 91
cranberry fruitworms – 73
cutting celery – 23–27, 106
cutworms – 62, 63, **92**

D

deer – 98
diatomaceous earth – 96, 97
"dirty dozen" – 13, 14, 83
diseases – 89, 99–102
    of apples – 17, 20, 99, 100, 101
    of blueberry – 73
    of celery – 26, 101
    of grapes – 57, 99
    of kale – 82
    of lettuce – 78
    of peaches & nectarines – 44, 101, 102
    of peppers – 62–63, 102
    of potatoes – 69, 102
    of spinach – 50, 99, 100
    of strawberries – 36, 100
dish soap – 82
dolomite lime – 19, 43
dormant – 18–21, 40, 43, 44, 55
dormant oil – 95–97
drip irrigation – 56, 73
dwarf varieties – 16–17, 40, 43, 72, 76

E

elemental sulfur – 19
epsom salts – 104
Environmental Working Group (EWG) – 13
EPA – 83
espalier – 17

F

FDA – 12
fertilization – 103–104
    for apples – 19–20
    for blueberry – 72
    for celery – 25–26
    for grapes – 57
    for kale – 80
    for lettuce – 78
    for peaches and nectarines – 43, 44
    for peppers – 62
    for potatoes – 69
    for spinach – 69
    for strawberries – 35–36
fish emulsion – 19, 26, 35, 36, 44, 50, 62, 78
fish meal – 72
flea beetles – 50, 69, 73, **93**
floating row covers – 81, 82, 89, 92–95, 97, 102
fluorescent light – 34, 61
fusarium wilt – 50, 78, 100

G

grafting – 17, 43
graft union – 44, 45
grapeberry moth – 57, **91**
grapes – 53–58
gray mold – 73, 82
green june beetle – 44, 92
greens – 48, 77, 79
greensand – 62, 104
grow light – 34, 61
growing on – 62

H

heading cut – 21
heirloom varieties – 106–107
    apples – 17, 20
    potatoes – 66
horticultural oil – 82

I

insecticidal soap – 82, 95, 96
iron deficiency – 72, **104**
irrigation – 56, 73

J

Japanese beetle – 44, 92
june beetle – 44, 92

K

kelp – 35, 36, 45, 50, 103
kale – 79–82

L

lady beetle – 95, 96
lateral branches – 45, 46
leader – 21, 45, 46, 57
leaf curl – 45, 82, 102
leafhoppers – 69, **96**, 102
leafminers – 97
lettuce – 75–78
lime-sulfur spray – 95
lime fertilizer – 19, 35, 43
loam – 68

M

magnesium deficiency – 25
maggots – 81, 94–95
malabar spinach – 48, 51, 77, 106
manure – 25, 35, 52, 78, 80, 103, 104
mites – 20, 57, 87, 95
muscadine grapes – 53–58, 106

N

National Research Council – 12
nectarines – 39–46
neem – 92, 93, 96, 97
New Zealand spinach – 48, 50, 51, 106
nitrogen deficiency – 103
nutrient deficiencies – 103–104

O

organic matter – 80, 103
oriental fruit moth – 44, **90**

P

parasitic wasps – 81, 90, 91, 92, 94
peaches – 39–46
pear blight – 101
pear psylla – 97
peat moss – 35, 43, 50
peppers – 59–63
perlite – 35, 43, 50, 61
pests – 89–98
    of apples – 19, 20, 90–92, 94, 95, 98
    of blueberries – 73, 93, 98
    of celery – 26, 96
    of grapes – 57, 91, 95, 98
    of kale – 82, 91, 95
    of lettuce – 78, 95–98
    of peaches & nectarines – 44, 90, 92, 94, 95, 96, 98
    of peppers – 62, 91, 96, 98
    of potatoes – 69, 93, 98
    of spinach – 50, 93, 97
    of strawberries – 36, 94, 97, 98
pesticides – 12, 83–87
Pesticides in the Diets of Infants and Children – 12
pesticide residue – 9, 11–13, 83–87
    on apples – 16
    on blueberries – 72
    on celery – 24
    on grapes – 54
    on kale – 79–80
    on lettuce – 76
    on peaches & nectarines – 40
    on peppers – 60
    on potatoes – 66–67
    on spinach – 48
    on strawberries – 30
pesticide tolerance levels – 11
pH (of the soil) – 35
    for apples – 19
    for blueberries – 72
    for celery – 25
    for grapes – 57
    for peaches & nectarines – 43
    for potatoes – 68
    for strawberries – 35
phosphate, rock – 62, 103
phosphorous deficiency – 103
phytophtora root rot – 75
pine bark – 43, 72, 80
pine needles – 72, 80
plum curculio beetle – 20, 44, **92**
plum pox virus – 45, **101**
pollination – 89, 104

    for apples – 16, 18
    for grapes – 54–55
    for spinach – 48
    for peaches & nectarines – 40
potatoes – 65–70
pottasium deficiency – 103
powdery mildew – 20, 45, **99**
pruning
    apple trees – 20–21
    grape vines – 57–58
prunus stem pitting virus – 45, **101**

R
rabbits – 98
raised growing beds – 105
residue – see "pesticide residue"
rhizopus fruit rot – 45, **100**
rock phosphate – 62, 103
root maggots – 81
rootstock
    for apple trees – 17
    for peach & nectarine trees – 43
root weevils – 73

S
safe handling of produce – 92
scab – 16, 20, 45, 69, **100**
scale – 73
slugs – 19, 39, 78, **97**
snails – 36, 68, **97**
solanine toxicity – 65, 66
sooty mold – 82
spinach – 47–52
stink bugs – 94
strawberries – 29–37
sulfur – 19, 72, 95, 99, 100, 104, 110, 111
sweet bell peppers – 59–63

T
tarnished plant bugs – 36, 44, **94**
thinning cut – 21, 45
thinning
    lettuce plants – 78
    peach & nectarine fruit – 45
    spinach plants – 49
thrips – 44, **96**
tobacco mosaic virus – 60, 62
Total Diet Study – 12
tufted apple bud moth – 44, **91**

U
USDA—U.S. Department of Agriculture – 11, 12
USDA Plant Hardiness Zones (grow zones)
    for peaches & nectarines – 40, 42
    for potatoes – 67
    for strawberries – 31
U.S. Environmental Protection Agency – 11, 12
U.S. Food & Drug Administration – 12

V
vermiculite – 34, 35, 50, 61
verticulum wilt – 45, **100**

W
wilt (fusarium & verticulum) – 31, 45, 50, 78, **100**

X
X-disease – 45, **102**

Y
yellow jackets – 98

Z
zinc deficiency – 72, **104**

About the Author

Barbara Barker traces her love for gardening back to fifth grade when she started a business rejuvenating her mother's ailing plants and selling them back to her for a small profit.

Barker expanded her knowledge of plants by working in garden centers in high school and college. After obtaining a BA in English from the University of Florida, she started an internet company selling gourmet varieties of vegetable and herb plants.

A certified master gardener, Barker operates Gourmet Gardener from Florida where she lives with her husband, Richard, and two children, Rhett and Brian.

Author Online:

www.gourmetgardener.com

Also from Prairie Oak Publishing:

Growing and Using Stevia:
The Sweet Leaf from Garden to Table with 35 Recipes

Growing Stevia for Market:
Farm, Garden, & Nursery Cultivation of the Sweet Herb, Stevia rebaudiana

www.growingstevia.com

www.prairieoakpublishing.com

www.ingramcontent.com/pod-product-compliance
Lightning Source LLC
LaVergne TN
LVHW081354060426
835510LV00013B/1814